#IsHeHereYet

BEING THE PERSON YOU WANT TO BE WITH

TONY ORTEGA, PSY.D.

Printed in the United States of America

First Printing, 2017

Book Coaching & Editing: Alisia Leavitt, alisialeavittmedia.com

Cover & Interior Design: Amber Rochelle Hargett, behance.net/AmberHargett

ISBN 978-0-692-96337-1

Ortega Psychology PLLC
Antonio Ortega
16 Court Street Suite 2405
Brooklyn, NY 11241

www.DrTonyOrtega.com

FOREWORD

"Of all the creatures of earth, only human beings can change their patterns. Man alone is the architect of his destiny. Human beings, by changing the inner attitudes of their minds, can change the outer aspects of their lives."

- William James

In the history of man, there has never been, nor will there ever be, a demographic of people quite like the gay man. Unique in our history, culture, and shared experiences, gay men are a delicate and distinct blend of pride and pain, confidence and shame, success and failure, and most importantly, love and fear. Put simply, gay men are a beautiful and miraculous contradiction.

As a community, we have seen amazing progress and evolution in our fight for equality. Gay marriage, once thought a pipe dream, has come to fruition in recent years. TV and movies have begun showing a more accurate depiction of gay men as confident, intelligent, loving, and also as additives. Societal acceptance is on the rise and our younger generations have never grown up in such accepting environments. Indeed, some would say there has never been a better time in history to be gay.

But with that said, our struggle for full equality and acceptance rages on, and the pain and damage of being gay in an unaccepting world continues to traumatize many of us. So for all of these victories, many of us remain unfulfilled. We have disproportionately higher rates of depression and suicide than our heterosexual counterparts, and we seek outward and often unhealthy ways to garner acceptance and validation from the outside world, such as material wealth, drugs, and promiscuity.

And it is in this understanding that this book was created. The long held societal belief that love and happiness is found outside of ourselves is a horrible myth. It's a thief in the night that robs us of the opportunities to evolve and seek happiness from our one true source...ourselves. This book was written to create consciousness in the gay soul. To help our gay brethren move past the walls of fear, shame and guilt that surround and isolate so many of us, and to wake up to a beautiful new reality; one grounded in courage, vulnerability, self-acceptance, and self-love.

As a spiritually minded gay man, I see my own personal pain and struggle reflected back to me in both Tony's personal story and in the stories of the clients he speaks about, in anonymity, in this book. As a certified professional coach, I see the struggles and hardships of my clients powerfully represented in these pages. As gay men, we are all connected and our struggles are intrinsically linked. It is our shared experiences that make the gay community so powerful and resilient.

I invite you to see your story in the pages of this book and use this connection and commonality as a means to propel yourself forward into radical acceptance and healing. For it is only when we truly love and accept ourselves that we can truly love and accept others. The journey to a powerful, loving and intimate relationship with another begins with us.

Tony fills a large void in the resources available to gay men by writing this book. One created for spiritually minded, or at least spiritually seeking, gay men looking to move past the shame and guilt that prevents them from making intimate and loving connections with other gay men.

Although this book was written for gay men, by a gay man, I see lessons and a journey of self–acceptance, self-compassion, and self-love that anyone can take, as we all have our own unique blend of struggle and pain. Although our struggles, as human beings, can be very unique, our shared pain, as a species, is very real. If you happen upon this book, it is probably with good reason and I encourage you to use the wisdom and guidance contained within to move you on your own personal and unique journey of healing and self-discovery.

From my perspective, I see very few gay books that have tried and true, battle-tested tools gay men can use to better navigate the world around us, and how we show up in it. Add this book to your self-help arsenal. Return to it frequently to ground yourself in its wisdom and guidance. Read it to remind yourself how to unapologetically and powerfully show up in the world.

As gay men, we've made incredible progress in the past several years in legal and societal acceptance, now it's time to make progress in self-acceptance and self-love.

Through this book, I hope you find your way to your true self. Through this book, I hope you find your way home.

Sincerely,

Joel Readence
Tony's coach and friend

_____

INTRODUCTION

T hey say your deepest pain becomes your greatest purpose. And this pain was fucking deep.

The catalyst of this book was a breakup. It is ironic that a breakup influenced the development of a relationship book; or, maybe not so ironic. For centuries, artists have created beautiful things from unrequited love. A broken heart has been at the foundation of many of history's greatest masterpieces.

So, here is a little history: I pride myself on being a very accomplished man. Most of my endeavors are met with a great deal of success. However, there was one area that had eluded me most of my life: relationships. I was convinced I was doomed to be single—as every relationship with a guy I ever had ended in a disaster. I was so miserable being single that I would do everything in my power not to be single. When relationships ended, I did everything I could to avoid the pain. I thought I wasn't good enough for relationships.

I lived in this story for many, many years. As relationships kept failing, I would shake my fist at God, or see myself as "different" or "less than" because of it. This all led to me getting into some very dark places in my life.

The evening of Friday, November 2, 2012, I was sitting on the toilet in my apartment in Queens, half drunk on frozen margaritas, smoking a Marlboro Light, and arguing with my "boyfriend" over forty dollars. (I use the word "boyfriend" in quotations because it was a relationship he had no idea he was in.) At that moment, I woke up—with a deep knowing that this relationship was over. I felt so pathetic that I ended the conversation, took a long last drag off the cigarette, and knew something had to change.

5

I decided to take hold of the wheel of my life and change direction. Over the next couple of years, the right people, the right books, and the right programs came my way. While some bounced in and out just to jumpstart my spiritual path, others have remained, mainly my study of the metaphysical text *A Course in Miracles*. It was the teachings in this text, combined with my spiritual and metaphysical work, which led me to unravel the things I was using to numb out and begin to feel more alive.

After beginning my spiritual journey and immersing myself in *A Course in Miracles*, I decided to work with a life coach; someone who seemed to have the well-rounded kind of life that I wanted—including a wonderful relationship. A relationship was one of the things I had not yet been able to successfully work out at the time, maybe because I was avoiding, or too busy working on myself. Through my work with this coach, I was able to rewrite the scripts I had been living under for most of my life and dive head first into the dating pool. It was easy at first, and I still stumbled on many occasions as my dating muscles had atrophied quite a bit in the years that I had not exercised them, but I kept taking that next right step.

On March 3, 2016, I met Fernando, the man of my dreams (or so I thought back then). While we had been talking for months online, we had not met before our date. I turned him down for sex over and over again as I was initially not really into him. But I began to think he seemed to have all the qualities I wanted in a man, which is why I continued to hold off on a one-night stand. He was equal parts sexual and spiritual. He was gainfully employed and seemed as motivated to work on himself as I was.

Fernando even matched most of the qualities I had listed in my "Manventory" I had completed New Year's Day 2016 (more on Manventories later). I figured, *Let's meet and see what happens.* When I first met him, I was like, *Homeboy photographs a lot better than he looks in person.* After chatting with him for a while over drinks and then ending the date with an intense make-out session in the streets of New York City, I was smitten.

However, there were some speed bumps along the way. He was dealing with some personal issues that I felt would get in the way of anything blossoming from our union, but something told me to give him a chance. I made myself wrong for feeling this way and dove in with my eyes closed. We had a lovely relationship that lasted sixty-nine days. It wasn't perfect, but it broke my then eight-year dry spell, and I was in love.

After a few weeks, he even said, "I love you." This was thrilling because no one had said that to me in such a long time. I thought that I had achieved the prize from all my hard work since that fateful Friday night in 2012. I had learned my lessons from all my previous failed relationships and now found what I was longing for.

He even gave me the title of "boyfriend," which only lasted seventy-two hours before he decided to take it away.

I turned into a state of fear for the remainder of the relationship and he ended things quite abruptly on May 10, 2016. I was devastated.

For the next six weeks, I felt completely at a loss over what to do to manage the pain. I numbed it through alcohol and sex. When I was more rational, I searched the Internet for books on gay relationships and breakups, but everything was so out of date. My coach was very supportive, but he was still in his wonderful relationship, and I felt like I couldn't relate to him because he had what I wanted and but just lost. This is no reflection of his capacities as a life coach. On the contrary, the man is simply amazing. I just had to go through the emotions.

I decided that if there wasn't a good, up-to-date, dating and breakup book for gay men, then I would write it. I was fed up with the "single-to-relationship" books that were currently on the market. It seemed that all of these particular books were "do this and get the relationship." I decided it was time to write a dating and relationship book that was more along the lines of "do this, be the person, see what shows up." At the time of writing this book, I am still single and dating.

However, thanks to the lessons from my relationship with Fernando and every other ex, I've embraced the journey to be perfectly okay with who I am as a single man. This was the first step that I neglected for the majority of my life. Now I feel very strongly that I will be in that wonderful relationship. I've done the work on the steps that I teach you about in this book.

You may ask, "What is a single guy doing writing a book about dating and relationships?" I have asked myself that very same question; a question that stopped me from writing this book for some time despite being divinely inspired to do so. I write this book because it is something that I would want to read. While the result of a relationship may be what we are all looking for, the process to get there is just as, if not more, important.

A Course in Miracles says, "To teach is to learn." I opened myself up to the potential learning experiences that writing this book has brought to me. I am not suggesting that what I'm teaching is the only way and that all the other ways before this one don't work. I am suggesting, however, that this is a different way, so it may work differently.

Today, I am a student and teacher of *A Course in Miracles*. I like to refer to it as the "Course." It is a book of universal spiritual truths not based on any religion or dogma. I will be quoting from the Course (as well as from metaphysical teachers Gabby Bernstein and Marianne Williamson) on a regular basis throughout this book. I ask you to look at the teachings objectively and see how they apply to you.

If the word "God" or any other dogmatic term bothers you (and I can certainly understand how it could), feel free to change it to another term that resonates with you. I, too, was not a deeply spiritual person until I found my awakening in 2012. When I first came across the Course, the name Jesus bugged the crap out of me. I just changed it to Higher Power, and it was much more palatable for me at the time.

While I write this as a gay man and predominantly for gay men, I feel that the themes in this book are relevant to anyone regardless of sexual orientation. Don't let my sexual orientation throw you off from incorporating the principles in this book. You can easily change Grindr to Tinder, or swap out any other terms and pronouns that don't apply to your sexual orientation. The results will be the same.

As I wrote this book, it became less of a "how to" manual and more of an experiential journey. While you work on the lessons of this book (especially in the first eight chapters), I encourage you to remain single and focus on your growth. This does not mean you should complete these chapters in a week (although, I would be tempted to). I will point out some things to consider; I call them "Miracle Moments." Make sure you pay special attention to these Miracle Moments in every chapter.

I also suggest that you keep a dedicated journal for the work you will do along this journey. Each chapter ends with a "Makeover Moment" and exercises, as well as meditative affirmations to make the experience more personal. You can also keep track of your insights in your journal as you navigate through this liberating process of *being* the person you want to be with.

The names and details of the individuals I talk about throughout the book (my exes, as well as clients) are changed to avoid disclosing any personal and identifiable details to protect confidentiality.

The most important message that I want to leave you with is: Who do you want to be, regardless of your relationship status?

And now, I present to you *#IsHeHereYet: Being the Person You Want to Be With.*

- Dr. Tony Ortega

————————————

1

GETTING TOTALLY OKAY
WITH WHO YOU ARE

"Life is a journey and it's about growing and changing and coming to terms with who and what you are and loving who and what you are."

- Kelly McGillis

For most of my life, I have judged myself as "less than" because I was single and perceived myself to have the most difficult time in dating and relationships. I would look at others and see how they navigated dating and relationships with such ease; I knew that there was something wrong with me.

Because I thought that there was something wrong with me, that was what I manifested. I alternately manifested long periods of being single, and the most emotionally unavailable men. When I did come across emotionally available men, I didn't know what to do with them. It was as if someone had asked me to build a nuclear missile. I was clueless.

I can likely trace my lifelong pattern of not accepting myself to a very early age, primarily to being gay and struggling with my sexual orientation. I knew I was different, almost from the word "go." I grew up in an era where being gay was barely out of the

American Psychiatric Association Diagnostic and Statistical Manual. Being gay was something only effeminate men were.

I felt different from my same-aged peers but could not put into words what that difference was. Starting in the sixth grade, I endured years of bullying. I was not a very masculine boy, nor interested in what the other boys were interested in (and to this day, I still hate sports). My nose was always in a novel or comic book to escape the reality of my life. My religious upbringing did little to help me through my feelings of insecurity, as I felt that I was doomed to hell because of my same-gender attraction.

As a teenager, I was coerced into having sex with a grown man. This left me feeling even worse about myself, blaming myself for allowing this to happen. While I'd started to acknowledge my same-gender attraction, I would not do anything about it for fear of ridicule and possibly being raped again. Shortly after that, the AIDS epidemic hit. Now, not only was being gay equated with being an abomination, but it also meant death. This forced me further into the closet and into a string of short-lived heterosexual relationships, drug and alcohol abuse, and chronic suicidal thoughts. The trauma from being raped and all my unacknowledged fears of being gay would lead to the unfulfilling relationships I would have in my later years.

At one point, I decided that having attractions would only lead to more trauma, bullying, and maybe even AIDS. I became the emotionally unavailable person that I would later date. I also recall not having any positive role models for emotionally available relationships, as divorce is an epidemic in my family (at last count, at least nine). Add to the fact that when I was growing up, gay men had no positive role models. I recall Rip Taylor from *The Hollywood Squares* and Liberace as the only ones who seemed remotely gay, but they were never really "out." I thank Neil Patrick Harris, Matt Bomer, Ricky Martin, and so many other celebrities today for positively emulating what being a gay man can be like.

Everyone around me knew I was gay, but I refused to acknowledge it. While I did have sexual interactions with men, it was usually under the influence of drugs and alcohol. I justified my sexual encounters with men by saying that as long as I stayed sober, I wasn't gay and I wouldn't have sex with men. I told myself it was the drugs and alcohol that influenced me to have sex with men.

It was not until after my father's death and my attending Gay Days in Orlando, Florida, when I was 29 that I was able to acknowledge to myself that I was gay. I saw two very masculine men holding hands and kissing, and I realized being gay wasn't about being effeminate or dying of AIDS.

Now, this was not the end of my low self-acceptance. I had to deal with body image issues, coming out at a "late" age, and ageism in my newfound community. I thought for sure I could now have a relationship, but that did not happen. After a short-lived relationship in 2004, a six-month relationship in 2005, and a string of very short-term and often one-sided relationships, I was still in the same boat as before.

Miracle Moment:
If I look back at my relationship history, whether female or male, they all have one thing in common: They were all emotionally unavailable in some way, shape, or form.

They may have been different genders, different shapes, different ethnicities, etc., but the people I dated never seemed to feel for me what I wanted them to. The way we show up to the world reflects back through our relationships and our experiences. I had become emotionally unavailable; therefore, I was with folks who were emotionally unavailable. This is why it is so important to *be* the person that you want to be *with*.

All of this led to the belief that I did not know how to do relationships. Since I had a total of three "official" relationships (one with a woman for eleven months and two with men for three and six months, respectively), I held on to the belief that I was not like other folks. I didn't do relationships. I even said so many times during my relationship with Fernando. He had been in several longer relationships. Because of my emotionally unavailable way of thinking, I had this undercurrent of inferiority around him because he was the "expert" in navigating the day-to-day stressors of an intimate relationship. Looking back, I think that it is funny that I viewed myself as inept to deal with an intimate relationship despite an eight-year dry spell before Fernando, as having a long string of relationships does not necessarily equate to being able to deal with intimate relationships.

After my relationship with Fernando, I had several sessions with my coach about what had gone "wrong" (my coach never said those words, mind you; I did). I heard myself tell him the same thing I would tell Fernando: "I don't know how to do relationships."

My coach said, "Well, let's take a look at all the relationships in your life today. You have amazing friends who show up for you in a strong way, as you show up for them. You have an amazing, thriving private practice that helps so many people lead spectacular lives. You do know how to do relationships."

He was right. I did know how to do relationships, despite what my fear-based ego mind was telling me. I was giving Fernando all my power, leaving me in a place of fear and emotional unavailability. Here is what I realized was important in being in a relationship:

I can love unconditionally.
I can walk through my fears.
I can share my vulnerabilities.
I can set boundaries.

I can communicate and express my feelings.
I can allow another person to be whom they are without
trying to rescue and change them.
I can think of someone's needs without sacrificing my own.

I also had to learn about who I truly am. This was one of the biggest turning points in my development as a person, as well as getting okay with who I am. Who I am is NOT based on whom I have for a boyfriend. Who I am is NOT what I do for a living. Who I am is NOT how much money I make or have. Who I am is NOT how many guys with whom I have sex. Who I am is NOT all those luxurious places I have traveled to.

Who I am IS the person I am to others. Who I am IS the love in my heart for my people and myself. Who I am IS what I contribute for the betterment of the world. Who I am IS the level on which I show up in the world. Who I am IS how I step into my power, despite any perceived or objective adversities. This is who I truly am.

What I gained from holding onto the self-limiting thoughts was that I was not accepting responsibility for my role in my singlehood. I was trapped in a state of separateness and emotional unavailability from others. The reason for holding on to this was to escape responsibility for my own life. I don't know if it was repressed adolescence or what, but I would point the finger at someone else or blame God before taking charge of my own life. Even today, I can sometimes stay in the very familiar zone of inaction. This zone breeds a level of comfort because it is what I know. I don't particularly like the phrase "comfort zone," as it really is not. The familiarity breeds comfort, so "familiar zone" is a better phrase to use.

Another factor was the thought that I was pressed for time, because of coming out at a late age and being an older gay man. My age and/or the fact that I came out later in life has always played a factor in me being desperate to escape my singledom. But time is irrelevant. The Course says that a miracle abolishes time. How? Well, something to know about the Course is that it is based on certain premises:

1. *Only love is real.*
2. *Miracles are a shift in perception from fear to love.*

When I am in a place of "my time is running out," clearly I am in a place of fear. However, when I shift my perception to that of love (and create a miracle), the race against the clock is abolished and I am free to be me. Whenever I have feared the clock ticking, I have made very poor decisions. I rushed into things for the immediate gratification of stopping the clock. I either stayed in relationships past the expiration date or went for having something right now versus waiting for that amazing connection.

Also, when I approach dating and relationships with the fear that I am running out of time, I approach it with a sense of lack. Somehow I lack something in my life and I need to fill it now. This is why I had only attracted filler boyfriends and lovers. Getting totally okay with who I am is recognizing that I am not missing anything. I am whole and I am complete.

What a relationship will ultimately do is add to my life, not complete my life. I have always disliked hearing people introduce their significant others as, "This is my other half." If I perceive my partner as my other half, that implies that I perceive myself as only a half person. Try instead walking around affirming to yourself that you are whole and complete and see what shows up in your life.

Once I made it my full-time work to get totally okay with who I am, I started taking charge of what it was that I wanted for my life. That didn't always guarantee the results I wanted, but it did allow me a sense of freedom from fear and emotional unavailability, as well as anger, resentment, blame, and self-loathing. This is such a remarkable place in which to stand. I get a lot more done when I am in this empowerment. In my work with clients, I have seen this manifest in different ways.

CASE STUDY

Don, the Man Who Couldn't Come Out of the Closet
&
Myles, the Gay Man Who Didn't Want to be Stereotyped and "Had to Do More"

In 2013, I began working with a young man, Don, who was in his 30's and was having difficulties coming out. He had never had sex with anyone (male or female) and could not say the world "homosexual" without turning fifty shades of red. Don was so preoccupied with what others would think of him if they knew he was gay. He was in an industry that typically is not very gay-friendly.

One of the main things I had to do with Don was to start the process of getting him okay with who he was. I guided him through self-acceptance instead of "other-acceptance." We can have all the acceptance from others in the world; however, while we continue to reject ourselves, the acceptance of others does not amount to anything in our journey. While it is certainly nice to have the approval of those around us, it is not a necessary ingredient in getting totally okay with who we are.

Another one of my clients, Myles, also had difficulty accepting himself as a gay man. He felt that being gay meant that he had to give up loving sports and to adopt a love of all things Cher. One of the first steps was to get him to understand that by identifying as a gay man, all this meant was that he was acknowledging his same-gender attraction. Everything else was more of a choice (yes, I am of the belief that homosexuality is not a choice). Myles realized that whom he was attracted to did not define what he liked to do in his spare time. However, it was not the last step in getting him totally okay with who he is.

Myles would sit in session telling me there was "more" he had to do. He felt that he had to be more open, and tell more people that he was gay. I confronted Myles on how this could be a delaying tactic by his subconscious mind to prevent him from getting to self-acceptance. Since he'd spent so many years in the closet, this became his familiar zone and a more comfortable place for him to be than openly gay. It took many sessions for Myles to realize his lack of self-acceptance was what was causing his discomfort, not that he wasn't "out" enough.

To get these two clients to be okay with who they are, I needed to help them recognize that identifying as a homosexual only meant that they acknowledged their same-gender attraction. Also, I reminded Don and Myles that while it is nice to have the approval and acceptance of those around them, it is not the necessary ingredient to being totally okay with who they are. Everything else was up to them.

Another concept from *A Course in Miracles* that helps me in this area is the notion that "The world of perception...is the world of time, of change, of beginnings and endings. It is based on interpretation, not on facts." What this means is that my perception of things is not necessarily the reality of the situation. My perception of myself can be based on false interpretations and not necessarily facts.

I find that it is easier to focus on what is wrong with me than to cultivate what is right with me. Again, by focusing on what is wrong with me, I get the opportunity to refuse responsibility, stay in my familiar zone, and not have to change. Why? Change can be scary. We don't know what will be on the other side. However, in my journey to greater self-acceptance, I realized even if I didn't know what was on the other side, it had to feel better than what I was feeling before.

Projection is often perception, as the Course also says. If my perception of myself is one of negativity and lack, then that is what my perception will find. Let me elaborate on this some more. Similarly, in social psychology, "confirmation bias" is the tendency to interpret new evidence as confirmation of one's existing beliefs or theories. It means I will look at and create situations that will confirm my existing beliefs. When I shift these beliefs to something that is more in line with who I truly am, that is what I will find.

With regards to shifting my beliefs about myself, I teach my clients—and practice myself—creating new beliefs that are realistic. Anyone who knows me knows I have this passionate crush on Channing Tatum. Yes, I can shift my beliefs to say I can bag Mr. Tatum, but that is not very realistic. Not because I am not good looking enough, but because he's happily married to a woman. However, I can shift my beliefs to reflect something like, "I can attract a gorgeous man regardless of my age or my past." *That* is something that I can buy into.

So you may be wondering, "What can I do to get totally okay with who I am?" You have heard my journey of getting totally okay with who I am; now it's your turn.

Each chapter will end with exercises. Use your dedicated journal to write down your thoughts and experiences on each of these questions to make this journey as personal as possible.

MAKEOVER MOMENT:

1. What lifelong stories have you been living in?

2. How can you rewrite these scripts?

3. What would the people you love and trust say about what you have in common with your peers?

4. What do you have in common with these individuals?

5. How are you viewing yourself as separate and different from others?

6. How do you benefit from holding on to the thought that you are different and separate?

7. What would be available to you if you let go of the thought that you are different and separate?

8. How can you shift your maladaptive beliefs about yourself to more realistic and adaptive ones?

9. What would these new beliefs look like and what is possible to create once you buy into them?

Here are some meditative affirmations that you can use in your quiet time/meditation practice to assist you in getting totally okay with who you are. Feel free to change them to make them more personal.

"I am complete and lacking nothing."

"I am defined by who I am in the world."

"I am not separate from others."

"As my perceptions change, so will the way I look at myself."

*"My past does not dictate the course of
my present and my future."*

"I am enough."

Do you see how you can now get totally okay with who you are? It can take some work to undo the years of self-flagellating behaviors that conditioned us to feel unworthy. The work is simple, but may feel difficult at first because it is different than what you are used to. It requires vigilance, perseverance, and maybe some accountability partners to help you on this journey.

Getting totally okay with who you are is the first step of this process. Let's take explore our perceptions of relationships and how they impact the way we show up for others and ourselves. Follow me as we explore "Stop Making Relationships Your Higher Power" in the next chapter...

2

STOP MAKING RELATIONSHIPS
YOUR HIGHER POWER

"Learn to enjoy every minute of your life. Be happy now. Don't wait for something outside of yourself to make you happy in the future. Think how precious is the time you have to spend, whether it's at work or with your family. Every minute should be enjoyed and savored."

- Earl Nightingale

Throughout my life, I placed more importance on being in a relationship than in discovering my core value. I looked around me and saw other people could get into relationships with much ease, or so I thought. I did not believe I had the same capabilities to do so. Every time someone didn't like me back, or a date did not lead to a relationship, I felt like there was something innately wrong with me.

Why could other people find a healthy and loving relationship with the person of their dreams and the only way I could seem to be in a relationship was with some troll I was not interested in? I could have been in a relationship anytime I wanted to--if I was not selective in my choice of mate. I have some standards, most of the time. This led to constant feelings of low self-worth, as I would constantly compare myself to my coupled counterparts.

I think part of this may have developed as always feeling like an outsider because I am a gay man, although I could not verbalize it back in the day. As I have come to learn throughout my life, many individuals feel like outsiders, regardless of their sexual orientation. Before I was able to acknowledge my same-gender attraction, I knew I was different. Being predominantly single just fueled this sense of separation from others. Yes, I performed great at school, and I had awesome people in my life, and I have all of these marvelous qualities about me. But none of these made me feel comfortable being single.

Miracle Moment:
Getting really comfortable with
being single makes all the difference
in the world and shifts your energy
in a whole new light.

When I am not okay with being single and not okay with who I am regardless of my relationship status, the universe reflects back my perception, and I create the reality of feeling separate and defective. The moment I relinquish the need to be in a relationship to validate my existence, my energy shifts and different things start to happen.

This is proven to me more times than not and I often experiment with the concept. On days I feel down on myself, I check dating/ hookup apps and get virtually no results or get results I don't like. However, on the days that I feel good and don't care what happens, the opposite is true. So even online, this concept works. Your energy will transfer regardless of the medium you are using to meet potential suitors.

Ever have a morning when things don't seem to be going your way? Your perception then picks up every little bad thing that happens and overlooks any good that may come your way. The same goes for not being okay with being single. I would constantly look at what I didn't have, instead of being grateful for what I did have and working towards achieving the goals I wanted. The reality is that being single is a choice, not a curse, and being single can be a gift.

As I mentioned earlier, I can easily be in a relationship and compromise what I want just for the sake of being in a relationship. Or, I can hold out for what I want. It's perfection versus connection. *Do I want to have that perfect relationship on the outside where I feel just like everyone else, or do I want that deeper connection with a soul? That's the big question.* The gift is that being single allows me time to work on myself and to a place where I can create what I want for my life and my future spouse. Having that time is truly a gift.

I have seen so many relationships fail because the people were not ready to be in a relationship. Now, let's not use "I am working on myself" to avoid romantic relationships altogether. What I am suggesting is that we use our single time to get ourselves in a place to create magic, and shift our energies to allow for that other person to just waltz in. This allows us to create the energetic shifts to not only manifest our ideal partner, but also to be wildly okay with who we are even if we are single.

I think that one of the main issues for me—and with clients that I have worked with—has been working through how society portrays single individuals, as well as the micro-aggressions we receive from advertising and media about being single. It has been my experience that rarely does media and advertising celebrate being single. Instead, it makes it look like a virus that needs curing.

In my interactions with other gay men, I would get flack for being single. One former supervisor would ask me every time we spoke if I had a partner. Another friend of a friend would ask within five minutes of seeing me if I was with someone yet. I would answer no, and he would give me this confused look and say, "But why?" These two examples—and more that I can list but will spare you—remind me how some people make relationships the end-all, be-all of their existence, and anything else comes secondary.

I feel that one of the reasons why I (and others; gay men in particular) make relationships our Higher Power is because it normalizes things. Gay men have the stigma of being perceived as promiscuous beasts that have sex whenever they want. While sometimes this is the case, promiscuity often is fueled by a sense of low self-worth. Relationships engender a sense of belonging and a feeling of being "just like everyone else." Ask anyone who belongs to a marginalized population the extents to which they have gone and will go to feel a part of something bigger.

Advertisements and TV shows rarely do anything to promote being okay with being single. You either see couples and/or propaganda geared towards getting to buy a product or service that will make you part of a couple. Rarely do you see product/service endorsements that say, "Hey, buy this product/service and you're going to be so okay with being single." Instead, we get, "If you buy this, you will get the boy/girl" or "this (being in a relationship) is what normal looks like."

I remember being a young child, watching *Mary Tyler Moore* and thinking to myself, *She's never had a real boyfriend on the show!* Yet she is probably one of the first examples in my life of how one can be single and very successful. However, my girl MTM is one of the few individuals successfully portrayed in mainstream media as single and powerful.

Despite media representation and the micro-aggressions in advertising to single people, I got to the point where I recognized my worth as a person, not merely as someone's husband or boyfriend, and that turned the tide in the situation. It happened because I was so tired of feeling like a mutant in the world that I had to continually rewrite the negative scripts in my head from which I was operating.

Miracle Moment:
Whether I am in a relationship or not,
the greater value is in who I am as a person
rather than whom I have at my side.

Statistics are not my favorite thing in the world; however, sometimes numbers can be very powerful in illustrating very objective truths. The US Bureau of Labor reported that in 2014, 64% of the population were reportedly single and not in a committed relationship. Also in 2014, it was reported that 50% of all marriages end in divorce. Guess I am not the outsider I thought myself to be after all...

One of the biggest hurdles I have overcome in my dating and relationship history is not making relationships my Higher Power. This concept came to me via something a client of mine said. He was talking about how he was making money like a god and I sat in my chair and thought to myself, *I make being in a relationship like my God.* When I connected the dots and realized that I was making dating and relationships my Higher Power, things began to shift. In my quest for love, I was so consumed by when was it going to happen that I neglected to be grateful for what was already in front of me, and neglected my self-care. When I embarked on a journey with a life coach to get to the heart of my "bad relationship" history (I am using quotations and will get to that later), I was still determined to get a relationship.

After several months of working with my coach, I felt the time had come for me to start dating again. I even decided to change up my typical choice of men (I usually go for younger and still do). Date after date, I became increasingly frustrated that nothing was happening. Come to find out, every time that I went on a date and the dude was a possible candidate, I gave all my attention and energy toward making it work. Once again, I was making getting into a relationship my Higher Power.

At the start of 2016, I decided to redo my "Manventory" with the list of qualities I am seeking in a mate. Shortly after that, I met a guy whom I had been chatting with on those lovely dating apps. His name was Fernando. We did not consciously get together with the notion of a relationship but we mutually saw the possibilities that existed for each of us. Fernando even met most of the criteria on my Manventory.

After a few weeks, I strongly suspected that things were not going to work out. I saw he actually didn't meet the criteria I had set forth for my ideal mate and for myself. However, since I was making relationships my Higher Power and I was determined to make this relationship work come hell or high water, I stuck it out. I stepped out of my power and turned my will and my life over to the care of this relationship for what it represented. Sixty-nine days later, the relationship was no more and I felt gutted. I thought I had failed once again. However, it was through this "bad relationship" that I was able to step into my power as a single man. It took a while to get there, but I learned an important lesson.

Miracle Moment:
There is no such thing as "bad relationships;"
only opportunities for growth.

This leads me to a notion I heard in a lecture back in 2004, after a very "bad relationship" ended with a man I will call Mick. The topic of the lecture was on relationships and the lecturer said: "No relationship is a failure." I was quite annoyed at this speaker, as she had not been in a relationship with Mick. She went on to say, "As long as you learned something from the previous relationship that you can then apply to the next relationship, the former relationship served its purpose." In other words, no relationship is bad at its core.

Many years later, I came across *A Course in Miracles*. It says that every relationship is an assignment. It also says it is not up to us that we learn; it is up to us whether we learn through joy or pain. How I have combined these two concepts to my romance life is as follows: I learn from every relationship. My perception of joy or pain determines how I will navigate my experiences.

After the sixty-nine day relationship, I was in anger and rage for several weeks and was quite miserable. Once I decided I was not going to be the victim here, I emerged much stronger as I got to realize that this relationship was my "starter wife" relationship after a very long and self-imposed dry spell. I learned how I made my relationship with Fernando my Higher Power and how this affected my self-care as well as being in my own power. This was the whole purpose of my relationship with Fernando and this was the learning assignment. Once I realized it, I was free to step back into my power, only stronger than ever before.

Before being in a relationship, I had to be the man whom I wanted to be in a relationship with AND consistently be that person in and out of a relationship. With Fernando, I walked into it as the man I wanted to be with. Once I thought I was losing the relationship—because he wasn't giving me what I thought I wanted—I stopped being that person. I compromised my values and let the relationship be my Higher Power. In a conversation post breakup, he even mentioned how strong I was when we first got together but how that changed over time. Our mates do notice these things.

Obsessing over outcomes led to me not practicing the things I have to do for myself to be a better me. Also, not being in my power within the relationship led to many poor choices and presenting myself not as I truly am. I have come to learn that I gained much by holding on to this maladaptive belief (as with any maladaptive belief). You may be wondering, "What would I or anyone else gain by making relationships my Higher Power?"

Miracle Moment:

By making relationships your Higher Power, you continue to play small, to play the victim, to not take responsibility for the actions and choices you make; and to continue to blame God and others for any "misfortune."

This allowed me to stay exactly where I was, in the space of fear and familiarity. It is in leaving the comfort of the familiarity that I can create change in my life.

I see that my interest in being in a relationship was my selfishness. I did not have altruistic motives to be in a relationship. The relationship meant that I would now be like everyone else. When I moved from the notion of being in a relationship for my own needs and focused more on the notion of being in a relationship to love and be loved mutually, things started to shift. As of the time of this writing, I am still single. However, I see how I've shifted to less emotionally unavailable men because I don't approach dating for the sake of completeness as much as I used to.

CASE STUDY

Dean, the Man with the DL Boyfriend

In my work as a psychologist and coach, I have also seen this happen with many of my clients. One client in particular, Dean, demonstrated how making relationships his Higher Power became a very maladaptive force in his life.

Dean came to me seeking help with a relationship. He had begun a relationship with a man who was on the down low (DL); a man who was not out to anyone and allegedly had intimacy issues. Dean perceived himself to be very unattractive due to body image issues. However, since his man was so attractive and didn't seem to care about Dean's perceived body issues, Dean was completely smitten and his entire life rotated around this man. However, Dean's boyfriend was unfaithful to Dean, as well as emotionally and physically abusive towards him.

This relationship became such a powerful force in Dean's life that he would come back to it time and time again. By holding on to this relationship, his life was consumed by either pleasing this man or with wondering what was wrong with him that his boyfriend would be this way towards him. Through extensive therapy and coaching, Dean was able to tell his DL boyfriend to take a hike and he has not heard from him since.

For those of you previously unfamiliar with the term "Higher Power," it is a term used in most Twelve Step programs. This usually refers to a power greater than you; a supreme being or deity or some concept of God. It is used in a very non-dogmatic sense. I chose to use the term Higher Power here to illustrate how I have elevated relationships to a power greater than myself in the past.

As I wrote this book—the first draft, anyway—I had two first dates scheduled for the upcoming weekend. Both guys looked great on paper (or rather, online), showed potential, and I was excited to meet them both. Once again, to teach is to learn. Both canceled the dates for various reasons. The old Tony would have felt incredibly sad, down on myself, and had a mental temper tantrum. Today, I just laughed at it because I see the synchronicity of writing this book and living what I am teaching all of you.

MAKEOVER MOMENT:

Let's look at the ways we make relationships a power greater than ourselves. It is important to be brutally honest here to free yourself from the restraints this behavior causes. You picked up this book because you want to be powerful. Don't hold back in your answers.

1. In what ways have you made relationships your Higher Power/power greater than yourself?

2. Energetically, how does it feel when you are making relationships your Higher Power?

3. What is manifesting in your life when you are in this energetic state?

4. What do you gain by holding on to this?

5. How can you reframe these thoughts into something more adaptive so that you can step into your power?

6. What are the messages you receive that make you feel uncomfortable with being single and how can you rewrite them to make them truly your own?

7. Look at the times you have been single. Where have the opportunities for growth existed?

8. For every relationship that didn't work out, what did you learn from it? What were the synchronicities?

Conclude your exercises with the following meditative affirmations. These can be used to strengthen the insights you have gained from doing the exercises in this and every chapter.

"I am comfortable in my skin."

"A relationship does not define me."

"I am single by choice, and my life rocks."

"Every relationship is an assignment."

"I learn from every relationship in my life."

"I am a powerful person."

Miracle Moment:
This is the second step of this process:
Stop making relationships your Higher Power.

Getting to the point where we are wildly comfortable with who we are despite our external circumstances is the greatest gift we can give ourselves and to our partner. This way of being allows us to step into our innate power so that we can make any task ahead of us a success. The first two chapters force you to take a hard but good look at who you are, how you perceive yourself, and how that manifests itself in the outside world.

Now, let's explore how to make peace with your past...

3

MAKING PEACE WITH
YOUR PAST

"The Past is over. It can touch me not."

- A Course in Miracles

We all have a past. For some of us, the past is something we look upon with shame and regret. When these are the predominant feelings associated with the past, our present and future become clouded with these same feelings. It paralyzes us from taking any steps in the present moment. Many times, it becomes a self-fulfilling prophecy, as we tend to relive by recreating the past into our present. This is so evident in relationships and played a big role in my relationship with Fernando.

In 2004, after that rather disastrous relationship with Mick, I lived in shame and regret because, in that relationship, I compromised who I was for the sake of being in the relationship. (I know this was a consistent pattern for me, hence why the last chapter is all about not making relationships your Higher Power.) Mick was a young and attractive man. I always credit him as being somewhat of a Ricky Martin lookalike. I met Mick right before he got out of rehab, which should have been my first red flag. He was also 10 years younger than me, which has always been appealing to me.

I was so smitten that someone that good looking would be into me that I didn't care.

At the time, I had seven years sober in a Twelve Step program. He had sixty days. I broke a cardinal rule in the program about dating someone newly sober in the program. As time elapsed, I saw that Mick had only gone into rehab to beat a DUI rap (his third, something else I didn't know initially). Once he "beat it," he went back to drinking. He was what I would describe as a Jekyll and Hyde alcoholic; one sip of alcohol changed him into a selfish monster.

I held on to my sobriety as long as I could. Unfortunately, around the same time, I also received news that I would be losing my very cushy corporate job. Facing the loss of the job and the potential loss of Mick, I decided it was okay to start drinking again so I could at least keep Mick. I was trying to keep something, as many of my friends had turned their back on me because I was in a relationship with an active alcoholic. The loss of my job, Mick, and my friends would be too much to bear, so I held on to Mick for dear life.

This led to a very tumultuous period in my life, one that took almost eight years to recover from. I decided to drink again so Mick and I would be together. This did not end well, and I threw away all my values and continued on a very dark path—mentally, physically, and spiritually. I never made peace with the fact that I had compromised who I was for the sake of being in the relationship. Later in this book, I will talk about the issue of making compromises in a relationship versus compromising yourself in a relationship.

My next relationship with Dean in 2005 was less tumultuous but equally painful. Dean was a rather closeted gay man and somewhat sexually repressed (I was somewhat repressed as well, so I am not going to put all the blame on Dean). Although he was very affectionate towards me and very supportive of my attempts to get sober again, this relationship was one-sided. Except for my sobriety, everything had to be his way. Who we were out to was up to his discretion. How we had sex was almost robotic, and again, he dictated it.

Because I had not made peace with the Mick situation, I allowed

Dean to be in control of the relationship. I felt so crappy about myself for what I had done that I wasn't assertive in the least. And I only had three months sober when I met Dean. I did not speak up until he fell out of love with me (if he ever was truly in love with me, I don't know; he never said if he did or didn't). I don't blame him because who would want to be in a relationship with someone who did not speak up and shrank in the face of adversity?

I am sharing these stories with you to illustrate the importance of making peace with your past, especially past relationships. In my relationship with Fernando, all the unresolved stuff from Mick and Dean surfaced. I would tell Fernando that I didn't know how to do relationships because most of my relationships were so short and chaotic. I was ashamed to give him any details.

When I felt I was losing him, I didn't speak up when things would go in an unhealthy direction. I questioned what I thought was right and wrong. How would I know? My previous encounters had led to painful consequences. I couldn't put myself through that again, so Fernando had full control after only a few short weeks in the relationship.

I viewed some of Fernando's actions as if he was acting like Mick or Dean. When I thought he was doing something without consulting or asking me, internally, it was Dean all over again. When I thought I was going to lose him, I became weak and almost compromised my values to keep the relationship, the way I had done with Mick. By not making peace with my past, I was often not present in my relationship with Fernando. This led to me reverting from a strong individual when we first met into a whiny and scared child when we broke up. (I don't put all the blame on myself for the dissolution of this relationship; just owning my side of the street.)

I have many regrets that I have operated from in the past: regret about having come out so late, regret that I spent so much time out clubbing and being promiscuous that I did not have a history of successful relationships, regret that I rejected those men who were more worthy of my time to go towards the emotionally unavailable ones, regret that I compromised who I was in my relationship with

Mick, regret about never speaking my truth to Dean, and regret that I became weak in my relationship with Fernando.

When I was willing to let go of the shame and regret, despite the pain of past relationships and life events, everything aligned in perfect order, which in turn ended regret. Each experience builds upon the last to make things better. Mick, Dean, and Fernando needed to happen, exactly how they happened, to provide me with the curriculum for success. There was a lot I didn't know about myself and how I wanted to show up in the world. These experiences taught me just how to do that. Any deviation from how they happened may have led to another disaster until I finally learned from the experience.

Have you ever experienced a lesson over and over again, and when you look back as to why it continually happened, you realized you didn't learn the lesson the first few times it was presented to you? I am sure you have. I feel very strongly that every experience is a lesson for growth.

Miracle Moment:
The same lesson will continue to show up in your life until you learn it.

My regrets are life lessons. I know that in future relationships, I have to make myself a priority and stick to my values. I know that I have to speak my truth, albeit in a way that is received by my partner as it is intended and not from a place of fear, hurt, anger, or self-centeredness. I know that I have to practice mindfulness, and being more present in my relationships. At the very least, if this is all I learned from these past regrets, I am further ahead today than I was yesterday.

In a discussion I had with Fernando shortly after our breakup, I recognized that despite the hurt and regrets, I am a better person as a result of the relationship and breakup. I am also a way stronger person. I know better what to do in future relationships by being more cognizant of how my thoughts about the past may interfere with the present. There is a divine order in everything, even the things we regret. I don't say that to minimize anyone's pain. On the contrary, I say this to transform pain into beautiful life lessons to make us stronger and better.

I did gain a lot by not making peace with my past. You may think this is a ridiculous notion, but any recurrent maladaptive thought or behavior has a secondary gain, which is why we continue to engage in it despite knowledge of the pain that it brings. By living in the past in my present, I got to stay exactly where I was. Are you starting to see a pattern here? Change is one of the scariest things in the world, and a lot of folks I know hate change.

Why do we fear change so much that we avoid it like the plague? Change usually involves the unknown. The unknown can appear to be scary because we don't know it. What if it's worse than what we are currently experiencing? Conversely, we may have such a low self-image that we fear success or failure.

We fear we may not achieve the change or fail miserably when the change does come. Along these lines, maybe we feel we are unworthy of positive change, so we sabotage it before or during the period of transition. We shoot ourselves in the foot before even taking any forward movement towards the direction we think we want to go.

Sadly, we often change despite our fears of the unknown when we have hit our emotional rock bottom. I am certainly grateful for my emotional rock bottoms, but damn, they are painful! Rock bottoms show me what I don't want, remind me of what I am capable of, and show me how I never want to be that person again if I can help it.

This also fits in well with the concept of confirmation bias that

I spoke about earlier in the book. When I am living my past in the present moment, my ego (fear-based) mind will look for only those things that already exist in my thoughts and feelings. That's why there was always a big joke amongst my friends that Tony's "type" was young and emotionally unavailable. I never made peace with my exes, which is why I continued to attract men just like them and reject the ones that were not like them.

Lesson #289 of *A Course in Miracles* states, "The past is over. It can touch me not. Unless the past is over in my mind, the real world must escape my sight." The only way that I am reliving the past in my present is when I have not let go of the past in my mind. The only way that history will repeat itself is when I make the past my present by keeping the past alive in my head.

My current belief about myself lets me know I have the power and capabilities to create *exactly* what I want regardless of what has occurred in the past. My past does not define me. It has given me the lessons and tools that I need to create a better present and future.

While some of these life events have been painful and I certainly wouldn't want to go through them again, I recognize their value in teaching me important things. I no longer wear my past as scars on my psyche but as medals signifying my victory. Our past reveals what we have been able to overcome and transform, not something to be used as fodder for self-flagellation.

One of the greatest lessons that I have learned from Marianne Williamson is the whole notion around the word "sin." I can tell you that my childhood religion did not make the sin a very positive nor empowering term. On the contrary, I thought I was sinning with almost my every thought and feeling. I was listening to a lecture by Marianne Williamson, and she said sin is actually an archery term. In the world of archery, sin means, "missing the mark." (I will admit that I had to look it up and see if she was telling the truth—and she was.)

This newfound conceptualization of sin and how it applies to life events in my past has allowed me to release a lot of shame and guilt around the things that have happened. I made many of my bad decisions when I was not in my "right" mind. I missed the mark. Just like in archery, I learn from how I missed the mark to get the mark better—if not on target—next time. This gives me the freedom to live more fully in the present and not regret the past while fearing my future.

I can look at how I overcame certain situations to define who I am, not the situations themselves. While the Mick situation led to a pretty dark eight years, I did do a lot of good because of my determination and drive. I may have missed the mark several times, but I nailed it other times. I continued my education and was determined to become a psychologist. Thanks to the situation with Dean, I know how important it is to use my voice and communicate my feelings and needs.

My relationship with Fernando gave me the inspiration to express my creativity in this book you hold in your hands as well the pursuit of other creative endeavors. I now feel more alive and powerful than I did when I was with Fernando. In essence, thanks to these regrets (or life lessons), I am more driven, determined, communicative, and creative.

Caution: I do not suggest that we use this notion of sin to justify or excuse our actions. I want to use this concept to help you better understand the possible reasons why certain things have happened and empower us to make better and more adaptive decisions that will lead to hitting the mark.

CASE STUDY

Ronnie, the Man Who Lived in the Past

I recently worked with a new client, Ronnie. During our third session together, we were discussing the notion of relationships. He was conflicted because he fell in love too quickly and when he met someone he liked, he had nothing to offer. It dawned on me that he was going through the very things I was writing about in this chapter. He was not okay with his past and verbalized many regrets from past decisions.

I engaged him in a dialogue about what being single said about him. Initially, he had difficulty answering the question (as can happen in most thought-provoking self-analysis). Then he recognized he viewed himself as "less than" for being single, as well as for not being able to accomplish more in his life. Ronnie was able to acknowledge that he did the best he could with what he knew at the time.

By not making peace with his past and the choices he made, Ronnie was defining who his essential self was by what he had done or what had happened to him—not by what makes him whole, complete, and a wonderful person, loved by so many.

I then took Ronnie on a journey of self-exploration. I asked him to not focus on what he had accomplished but on what it had taken to accomplish what he already had done in his life (which was a lot, by the way). Ronnie was able to identify values like perseverance, tenacity, and drive as his core strengths and values. With further exploration outside of the session, he was able to rewrite the scripts he had been operating under and get to a greater level of being okay with who he is.

MAKEOVER MOMENT:

It's time, my brothers and sisters, to let go of what isn't serving you anymore.

1. Identify the situations/life events/relationships you regret about the past.

2. Look at how these situations were the catalysts for creating positive change in your life.

3. How are you a better person as a result of these situations you regret?

4. What positive things about yourself are you able to identify as a result of recovering from this event?

5. How can you reframe these regrets into thinking about them as "missing the mark?"

6. Whenever you are confronted with a regret from the past, how can you switch it around to identify the curriculum you need?

7. Look at the fear of change. What are your fears around change? Success, failure, not being worthy of positive change?

8. When something from the past comes up for you, what are some ways that you can be more present?

Now that you have completed these exercises, take some meditative time to affirm what is true for you today. Incorporate these affirmations into your meditation and see how free you feel.

"The past is over; it can touch me not."

"Every life circumstance is a curriculum for success."

"I am worthy of positive change."

"History does not have to repeat itself."

"I learn from every relationship in my life."

"I am present and show up for my life in a powerful way."

Our past experiences can become an avenue to become the authentic person we want to be. Shame and regret only keep us stuck in the past. Look for the lessons in the experiences that you are feeling shame and regret over.

WHERE CAN YOU MAKE CHANGES IN YOUR LIFE TODAY TO MAKE YOUR TOMORROW BETTER? THIS IS HOW YOU MAKE PEACE WITH YOUR PAST.

Now that you have made peace with your past, it's time to look at how you think/act/feel in the present. Let's explore comparison and talk about how we can finally break the yardsticks we use to measure ourselves up against others.

4

STOP COMPARING

"Your playing small doesn't serve the world."
- Marianne Williamson

One of the problems with social media is that you get to know what your exes and former flings are doing with their lives, sans you. I know that when I have seen posts from various exes or past flings that didn't work out, my first questions are "Why him and not me?" or "Why am I the one still single?" If any of these questions pop into your mind, you are comparing yourself to others and devaluing your Essential Self. For God's sake, stop stalking your exes on social media (I should follow my advice, no?). People post on social media what they want others to see. This is not always reflective of their reality.

In my relationship quest throughout my life, I always compared myself to my peers. Part of this was growing up gay in the '80s and '90s, but the other part was never teaching myself the value of who I am as a person. It was like breaking out the yardstick and measuring myself up against my peers and the portrayal of who "real men" are in mainstream media.

The origin of shame for me started from a very early age. I always felt different than others. I was always an overweight kid growing up. I didn't like sports, so I was never physically active, despite my mother's attempts of enrolling me in Little League baseball and karate (God, I am so physically uncoordinated). So my self-esteem was tied to my body image issues. This is another issue that is aggravated by media and advertising. Plus-size models and "bears" may be a thing now, but it wasn't when I was growing up.

When that feeling of being different was the undercurrent of my life, the comparing ran rampant. Eventually, I did one of two things: I either isolated from others so they wouldn't notice the difference, or I would overcompensate to become more acceptable. I rarely followed what it was that I wanted for myself unless it was in the comfort of my room with my nose in a comic book. I learned to conform to the expectations of others as best I could.

As a young adult, thanks to drug use, I dropped some weight and became popular. However, my popularity was based on what I was able to provide for others and not because of who I was. The drug subculture is a venue in which one can sometimes achieve a level of approval from others as well as build confidence in oneself. Drug use in the gay community continues to be a widespread epidemic. This has also led to alarming rates of sexually transmitted infections (STI's), all in the name of being liked instead of liking one's self.

Comparing myself to others always involved shame. Whether it was the shame for being overweight, not being athletic, being single, or being gay (or insert whatever adjective or any other condition you can think of), I always found a reason to feel unworthy. I could have achieved the drop-dead gorgeous body or the athletic prowess of professional ball player or even had that amazing boyfriend. The bottom line remains that none of this defined me. I needed to make the journey to work through my shame and stop the comparing.

The most powerful thing I was ever able to do was to drop all expectations from others and begin the journey to find my path. I didn't always get it right, as evidenced by my years of drug and alcohol use as well as dysfunctional relationships. However, I learned from trial and error and never gave up. Once I recognized who I truly am (as discussed previously), the comparing dwindled significantly.

With regards to my sexual orientation, I was plagued with the idea that to be gay I had to be effeminate, have long hair, and work as a hairdresser (my family was in the beauty supply distribution business, so it wasn't a far-fetched idea). To be a *real* man, I had to love sports and bang as many girls as I could. When I stopped measuring myself against others, I lost the need for labeling. I was able to make sense of my own life without the need to call something for what it wasn't.

Another aspect of comparing ourselves with others involves societal labels. Dropping the need for labels is paramount in stopping the endless barrage of comparing ourselves to others. I am now completely comfortable in my identity as a gay man. I am a psychologist and coach. I love comic books and science fiction. I enjoy musical theater. And yes, I am obsessed with Idina Menzel, Patti LuPone, and Lady Gaga (but don't care for Bette Midler). While stereotypical to some, these are choices I make. I also enjoy all things spiritual and metaphysical. I don't enjoy sports at all but love the tight uniforms (wink).

Comparing and labeling appear to be a form of controlling our life experiences. If I look back at my life, one of the feelings I can remember is that I always felt powerless. I couldn't initially understand why I always felt so different. When I started to acknowledge my same-gender attraction, I still felt powerless because I did not have anyone in whom to confide. Instead, I would sit back and just compare myself to others. Weirdly, it made my internal experience make sense. By comparing myself to others and labeling myself as different, I didn't feel as powerless. I created a reality where, although I felt I had some semblance of control, I felt like absolute shit about myself. I felt separate, but at least not powerless in understanding the world around me.

Miracle Moment:
Who I am is my super power.
When I am in my right mind, I know
and feel empowered.

Today, I don't shrink in the face of other people and play small. When I am playing small, I do nothing for myself and those around me. I am much more effective when I step right into my power as opposed to being the shrinking violet.

What I gained from comparing was not having to take responsibility for changing the things I could change about myself and accept the things I couldn't. The recurring pattern I gained from staying in those maladaptive ways of being was one of taking zero responsibility. It was easier to stay exactly where I was because I didn't have to walk through my fears and change.

Here's the crazy thing: Shaming myself was so "normal" that I didn't know how else to live. What would accepting myself 100% even look like? The concept was so foreign to me that I didn't even know where to begin. The familiarity of comparison and self-shaming was easier to manage. I knew it, and it was like my best friend, albeit a very dysfunctional relationship. It was like telling myself to start walking on only one leg despite having two functioning legs. I didn't know how to do that. Mechanically, it appeared easy, but it was different than what I was used to.

The Course says we have only one problem, and that is our thoughts of separation from God. (Again, if the word God triggers something in you, switch it to something else.) The philosophy behind this is that we are all connected. I take this to mean that while we all have different physical shells, what connects us all goes deeper than our bodies. No one is more important or better than another in the realm of spirit. If we adopt this philosophy, we will find no need to compare ourselves to anyone else.

Most metaphysical texts will refer to a point in our lives in which we took a detour into fear. Most likely, this occurred when we started thinking to ourselves, *I am not as good as* _____. Don't worry so much about backtracking to when this occurred. The solution is to grab the yardsticks you use to measure yourself up against others, break them over your knee, and start to develop a new way of thinking in which you no longer play small and show up powerfully in your life.

Lesson #338 of the Course says, "I am only affected by my thoughts." My thoughts of separation and feeling "less than" were what created a miserable experience and my pattern of dysfunctional relationships. I had to do the work of recognizing my value as a person and equal to those around me. Certainly, not seeing myself as an equal led to the deterioration of many of my past relationships. Once I changed my thoughts about myself and how I saw the world, my reality changed significantly.

Neuro-linguistic programming suggests, "Projection is perception." This line is just so pertinent in any discussion on self and relationships. As I walked around feeling unworthy and separate from others, the universe mirrored it to me. I attracted men who verified my separateness because that is what I was projecting onto the world. I saw myself as separate—and so did they. Once I changed my internal dialogue, the experience changed significantly.

With Mick, Dean, and Fernando, I know that this played a role in the termination of our relationships. At the point that I thought that I was going to lose them, I did not stand in my power as an equal partner in the relationship. Instead, I dug my claws into the door frame to salvage the relationship. These attempts to maintain the relationship at any cost finally led me to a series of emotional rock bottoms. However, I realized that when I felt that I was losing a relationship, I needed to step into my power and know in my heart that they were just as lucky to be with me as I was with them; not to hang on to dear life in a desperate attempt to control the relationship.

The thought of losing a relationship can send us into a spiral of self-doubt and comparison once again. We think to ourselves, *I didn't do enough* or *I am not good enough.* We believe that our lives are over and we will never love this way again (cue the Dionne Warwick song). Take other people off that pedestal, folks. We can stop separating ourselves from others and recognize that our partner is learning from this experience as well, despite their outward presentation of not caring. This levels the playing field and stops the incessant need to compare.

Comparing and playing small also plays a role in nonromantic relationships. I remember when my good friend John and I decided to teach a workshop together. While I was initially very motivated to teach about my favorite book, *A Course in Miracles*, I felt doubt about working with John. He is younger than me, better looking than me (in my opinion), and has not gone through the "dark and dirty" stuff that I have. However, because of who he is, I always felt like his equal, not his dark and dirty sidekick. When I was able to move past my comparison, I taught like a champ, and it felt so empowering. When I was in my comparison mode, my ability to teach was impaired. I played small once again.

Some other examples of comparing myself to others in nonromantic relationships occurred the weekend I was working on this chapter. I went to an event run by a spiritual woman who has thousands of devotees around the world. They wait on hours-long lines just to receive a hug from her. When I entered the event facility, I felt the positive energies all around. After some time, I started to shrink, and it was so unconscious that I didn't realize I was doing it until I was feeling sad and on the verge of tears.

Since I knew virtually nothing about this woman and I was surrounded by hundreds of folks who knew of her more than I did, I started feeling like I didn't belong; that I was not worthy. This brings to mind the notion of being in touch with ourselves and how it feels to be in our power, so that way when the comparing comes into play, we can recognize its draining potential and do something about it. Comparison is the thief of joy and pleasure in our lives.

The very next day, I attended a comic con. For those of you who don't know me, I am a huge comic book/science fiction geek. Whenever there is a comic con that I can attend close to me, I am there. I enjoy attending these events so much. One, in particular, is memorable: a comic con in New Jersey during the July 4th weekend of 2016. I had such a blast, more so than at any other con. Coincidentally, it was the same weekend I was working on this chapter. A good friend of mine, Emily, noticed how chipper and rejuvenated I was. I thought about it and came to a remarkable conclusion.

One of the main reasons that I love comic cons is because they are the one place where I know that I will not be comparing. Comic cons tend to be all-inclusive. All people from all walks of life go there. We all have one purpose; whether we are *Star Wars* fans or *Doctor Who* fans, we are there for the love of the fandom. It doesn't matter whether you are gay or straight, male or female, overweight or skinny, black or white. I don't break out my measuring stick because there isn't any need to. We are all there for the love of the genre. This led me to my new assignment, which was to duplicate this attitude in all walks of my life. This skill is easily generalizable to any area of my life.

CASE STUDY

Michael, the Man Who Compared Himself and Destroyed His Life

I worked with a client for many years by the name of Michael, a lovely young man who came from a nice family. He was the younger of two siblings. Michael grew up with a sense of separateness his entire life. An emotionally absent father did not help the situation any.

Michael always knew that he was gay but could never speak about it. As many young gay boys do, they followed the dictates of their families to fit in. Michael's family wanted him to be an athlete, so he tried playing sports, which he hated. He compared himself to his peers as well as to his emotionally absent father.

As he grew up, Michael pursued a career in which he had no real interest because he thought it was expected of him. Throughout his professional career, he grew to hate his work and to resent life in general. Eventually he did come out of the closet, entered a relationship with a man, and even bought a house with him.

Sadly, Michael's undercurrent of self-loathing led him to destroy his life subconsciously. He engaged in illegal activities, subsequently got arrested, and lost his job, home, and relationship. He came to me for coaching, and the work began. He started to realize how his own self-loathing led to many bad choices. He became very comfortable in his sexual orientation and even pursued a career that was more in alignment with what he wanted, not what others expected of him. Throughout his work with me, he climbed the ladder at his job and began a relationship with a man that was authentic. He was finally happy because he stopped comparing and labeling. He ended his thoughts of separation from others.

Miracle Moment:
Comparing – the act in which we minimize who we truly are and rob ourselves of any joy – essentially destroys our lives.

MAKEOVER MOMENT:

Are you tired of the comparing? Do you want to recognize your greatness and walk fully in your power? Break out your journal and answer the following questions so you can break the yardsticks of comparison in your life.

1. What are the areas of your life where you find yourself comparing the most?

2. What is the dialogue in your head when you are comparing?

3. How can you shift the dialogue from one of separation and exclusion to unity and inclusion?

4. Where can you see the similarities between you and others instead of the differences?

5. How does it feel in your body when you are comparing?

6. What would it (or how does it) feel in your body when you are not comparing?

7. How can you walk through life acknowledging your uniqueness as well as connectedness?

8. What could owning your power 100% possibly look like? (Play with this one a little, folks. There are no wrong answers.)

> **9. How can you get off the highway of chronic fear and practice more love and acceptance in your life?**

Once you answer these questions, celebrate your greatness by engaging in the following meditative affirmations:

"I do not play small."

"We are all one."

"Owning my greatness 100% is my natural state, and it feels so good."

"I step into love and leave fear behind me."

"Comparing myself to others is unfair to them and to me."

WHEN WE DROP OUR MEASURING STICKS, WE DISCOVER THE INNATE BEAUTY AND POWER THAT IS IN ALL OF US.

It is not in some of us, but all of us. Seeing how comparison steals your happiness and strips you of any power is the first step. In essence, we created these comparison scales. Therefore, we can also dismantle them. Go towards a path of love, no matter how scary it is, and you will end the endless comparison that drains you of all the awesomeness that is you.

You have done a lot of work on yourself, no? You are hopefully starting to see who you are and not what your fear-based mind tells you. In the next chapter, you will get crystal clear and identify what you want in a relationship.

5

GETTING VERY CLEAR
ON WHAT YOU WANT

*"You get to choose what you want, but you must
get clear on what you want."*

- Rhonda Byrne

As a mental health professional, a classic assignment I give to my clients is to make a grocery list of the ideal qualities you want in a mate. However, what I have come to learn is that it doesn't just stop at making a list. There are a few steps that follow.

One Sunday afternoon in February, I was attending church services at Unity on the Bay in Miami, Florida. Since it was Valentine's Day, the pastor was giving a sermon on love and relationships. He proceeded to ask, "You know when therapists give you that assignment to write a list of what you want in a romantic relationship?" I started to shrink into my seat, paranoid someone would psychically know that I was a mental health professional. The pastor continued, "By all means, make that list. Then you become that person and see what shows up."

I carried this message with me for many years, but didn't do much about it for a long time. I made this list many times but never "became" the person because I made relationships my Higher

Power. I had also not done the work to make peace with my past and get okay with who I was.

How could I become the person I wanted to be with if I had not done the work? It couldn't happen. To attract the man I wanted to be with, I had to be the man I wanted to be with. This was a major epiphany in my dating life that I came to after the dissolution of my relationship with Fernando.

Miracle Moment:
Being the man that I want to be with means I believe myself to be whole, complete, and lacking nothing.

In one of the many lectures by my good friend Gabby Bernstein that I have attended, she said something that added to the equation of getting very clear on what you want. She spoke about the Law of Attraction and how some people get the whole notion wrong. It's great that I wrote that list and then became that person; the missing part of the equation was that I had to *feel* what it would be like if I had it.

It was also great to identify I wanted to be with (for example) a fit and spiritual man and to be a fit and spiritual man, but if I couldn't get in touch with what this would feel like, I was leaving out an essential part of the equation. How would I know when what I wanted arrived if I didn't have a clear understanding of what my ideal mate's presence would feel like?

I decided that it was time to clean house. I was over my dating and sexual experiences from the past few months. I decided it was time to revamp the list. The one thing I can say was that I was really into being the man I wanted to be with, as far as my behaviors. However, I had not revamped my list in quite some time. On January 2, 2016, I sat down and wrote out my list again. I took it into my meditation and got in touch with what it would feel like to be with the man described on the list.

A few months shortly after that, I took a Pilates class with my friend John, and we had brunch. I texted Fernando as we had been texting and chatting online for a few months at this point, but had never met. We happened to be in the same area at the same time and decided to meet up for a drink. Initially, from his pictures and our conversations, I wasn't sure how interested I was in him.

After meeting him and speaking to him for a bit, I felt the attraction, and that is how our sixty-nine day relationship began. Here is the scary part (and the reason why I include this story here): When I reviewed my inventory list, I saw Fernando met most of the qualities except one. Ironically, he too had made a list, and I met many of the qualities on it except one. The formula worked. However, there was one catch.

While making the list, I avoided noting certain personality traits that would have led to a more successful relationship with a man. There was a certain sense of fear about putting down and then getting in touch with the feeling of what I wanted. The items I'd avoided would have led to a more successful relationship; however, this notion was still too scary to fathom. Again, fear of change.

I had been able to develop a certain level of comfort, familiarity, control, and self-centeredness in being single. I got what I had written down—but I had aimed small. In hindsight, I had excluded what I wanted to have (and be) in an ideal mate. Fear prevented me from being powerful in identifying what I wanted.

Sadly, Fernando was missing some very important things, but they were not on my list. Again, I am not putting all the blame on Fernando for the dissolution of our relationship as I had my role to play as well. I feared failure, success, vulnerability, and breaking up. I was doomed from the word "go."

What I do want to emphasize is the importance of getting very clear on what you want. Your inventory list may need several revisions. I would avoid things like exact height and weight. I would focus more on what would make this relationship as successful as possible based on the more mental, emotional, and spiritual traits. After that, you can add the physical stuff as that is important as well.

For this chapter, I would like to include my Manventory from January 2, 2016 (months before I met Fernando):

- Spiritual
- Sexual
- Health conscious
- Romantic
- Physically demonstrative
- Emotionally demonstrative
- Educated
- Legally employed (there's a whole story behind this one)
- Emotionally stable
- Emotionally available
- Working on himself
- Good endowed (as opposed to "well endowed." Don't want to get too specific.)
- Versatile (sexually)
- Responsive to my needs
- Open minded
- Doesn't do drugs
- Emotionally monogamous
- Sexually adventurous
- Physically active
- Emotionally aware
- Open-minded about my hobbies

For the most part, Fernando met a lot of these criteria. However, I did need to get much clearer in future Manventories if I was to attract what I wanted. I also needed to get very clear on what it would *feel* like so I could recognize it on a whole other level.

Another obstacle in identifying what I wanted and what I thought it would feel like is that I had no models for healthy relationships. With an epidemic rate of divorce in my family and no real gay couple models to follow, getting in touch with what I wanted was daunting. I had to go with my gut more and just pray I was headed in the right direction. God knows I have now figured out what I don't want, based on my experience.

I always encourage my clients to look at how they are benefitting from maladaptive behaviors, and I need to practice what I preach. For most of my life, I was never clear on what I wanted in a relationship. Why? I never viewed relationships for their intended purpose. Instead, I viewed relationships as a means of feeling normal, as well as a sense of accomplishment. Relationships were never really about sharing my life and my love with someone, but about being just like everyone else. This led into another part of getting very clear on what I want, which was redefining what relationships meant to me and for my life. Today, relationships are about two people coming together for love.

Miracle Moment:

When I realized that relationships were not my Higher Power and that I was whole and complete being single, I was able to start making the shift into a new concept of what a relationship was.

An interesting thing has been happening as I have started each chapter of this book. I know at the start of the week what chapters I will be working on. Before I began to write this chapter, I was chatting it up with two guys on dating apps. In the spirit of full transparency, I had set up meetings with these chaps for sexual purposes, not for romantic dates.

As the universe would have it (and as the Course says, "To teach is to learn"), both of these gentlemen ended up canceling on me. In the past, I would think it was because there was something wrong with me. Today, I know that it is the universe giving me the lessons I needed to have at the right time. I had a good belly laugh when it dawned on me how much the universe does have my back with regards to staying clear on what I want.

Miracle Moment:
Getting very clear on what you want is to have your intentions and behaviors be as consistent as possible.

Do I want to be in a meaningful relationship? Then I need to get the F off of Grindr. I can't find the love of my life if I am busy slinging my unmentionables across the five boroughs of New York City. Also, I have to be the person I want to be with, so I have to do the daily work on myself. This means I can't neglect my self-care to focus on endeavors that will not yield the results I want. When we become aware of the areas of our lives we have been neglecting, it's time to work on those first. This is the universe's way of saying, "Hey, you may want to work on this first before doing what you are obsessing on."

To add to the notion of being consistent with your intentions and behaviors, I want to tell you about my turning away from this just three weeks into dating Fernando. It was the weekend of the Tony Awards, and I had slept at his house that Friday night. During some pillow talk the next morning, Fernando said something to the extent of, "I don't need a label to know we are essentially boyfriends." You can only imagine how excited I was that I finally had a boyfriend after eight years.

Tony Awards night came along, and his house was packed with guests. Now that we were official boyfriends (although he told me not to tell anyone or change my relationship status on Facebook), I just cuddled with Fernando and drank copious amounts of wine. The details are a bit foggy (thanks, Cabernet) but Fernando and I got into an argument and he basically said we were not boyfriends and that he wasn't ready for a commitment. Fear took over, and I gave Fernando all my power in an effort to change his mind and keep him. I stopped being consistent with my intentions and behaviors as a result, and I feel that this was a large part (on my end) why the relationship ended. I stopped being the person he fell for.

I stopped being the person I wanted to be with.

Making this comprehensive (yet not concrete) list, being the person on this list, and then being in the feeling of the result is in line with this. By practicing these steps, I can be sure of more adaptive outcomes. If I am certain of an outcome (i.e., knowing there is a divine order to the universe), I can be part of my own process without making myself nuts. That's the hard part, but certainly necessary to manifest the relationship you want. If I follow the three steps but still feel anxious, I am blocking the energy for manifesting by worrying it won't happen.

One of the things I would suggest you do is to focus on a personal development endeavor while you are "waiting." This book has been all about personal development for me, teaching what I need to learn to create what I want for my life. If you are anything like me, you are so consumed with the whole notion of dating and relationships that other areas of your life have fallen by the wayside. It's time to work on you so that you become the person you want to be with. That way, you can focus on the feeling of what it would be like and make your personal life that much better.

CASE STUDY

Sam, the Man Who Thought He Was Clear on What He Wanted

Several years ago, I had the pleasure of meeting Sam, a young gay man in his late 20s living in New York City. Like all of us who come to NYC, he had dreams. Not only did Sam want to be a performer but he also wanted to be involved in a healthy relationship. However, Sam was going about it the wrong way. In between jobs, he would spend hours upon hours cruising the hookup apps on his phone instead of engaging in activities that would produce this healthy relationship he thought he wanted. It was almost addictive.

I engaged Sam in a discussion on how his excessive use of apps was likely a control strategy. He was feeling out of control in several areas of his life. However, he could assume complete control over how much time he dedicated to the hookup apps. The meaningless sex was a substitute for the love he was seeking. It was like using substances to medicate feelings. When Sam got to the point that he could channel his sense of powerlessness in a much more adaptive fashion, things started to change.

Sam started the process of getting an idea of who he wanted to be in a relationship with, as well as matching his behaviors to his intentions. As he got clearer on what it was that he wanted (beyond the physical and sexual), I encouraged him to be more of the man he wanted to be in a relationship with. Additionally, I enforced the notion of being consistent with his behaviors and his intentions. As he did, his use of the apps decreased more and more. He got clear on what he wanted and his behaviors began to match his intentions.

About a year or so later, he started dating a man who met much of the criteria Sam set forth for himself, and they have been in a relationship ever since. Although the relationship has not been without its issues (as no relationship is perfect), he has been able to stay in it and create what he wanted for himself in the area of love and relationships while enjoying a healthy sex life with his boyfriend.

Let's chat about sex for a moment, shall we? I am not saying meaningless sex is wrong. All I am saying is that if your intention is to be in a loving relationship, having sex for the sake of having sex is incongruent with your stated goal of getting very clear on what you want. If you want to have sex and not be in a relationship, then by all means do it. However, if your intention is to be the person you want to be with and channel that relationship, you may want to question your motives behind engaging in meaningless sex.

This reminds me of something that happened recently, a story I will call "A Numb Tongue, Lycra Mask, and An Empty Bottle of Wine." As I've said, when I started this book, the exact lessons I needed to learn have been provided to me. One morning, I was checking my lovely apps despite my better judgment, and some dude messaged me. It was 6 a.m. and guys on the apps at that time were either early birds like me or still high from the night before. I asked him which category he fit in, and he said the former.

When we met up later that night, he was high as a kite, wore a black Lycra mask with only a mouth opening in it, and drank most of my wine. My reward was a numb tongue—courtesy of the drugs he was likely doing that transferred to me somehow—as well as mediocre sex and an empty bottle of wine. If this story does not convince you to get very clear on what you want, I don't know what will.

MAKEOVER MOMENT:

Are you ready to get very clear on what you want for yourself and your future mate? It's time to grab your journal. Let fear take a back seat while you write down what you want in a mate as well as what it would feel like to have this kind of mate. At the end of it all, get in touch with you being this person and embodying these qualities.

1. **If you were to make an inventory of what you would like in an ideal mate, what would the list consist of?**

2. **What are the self-imposed obstacles to you being more like the person you want to attract in your life?**

3. **How can you get in touch with the feeling of what you want?**

4. **How can your behaviors be more congruent with your intentions? Or, how are your behaviors out of alignment with your intentions?**

5. **What areas of personal development have you been neglecting?**

* Take a deep breath in and then slowly exhale. Say: "I am the Light." Imagine yourself covered in brilliant light.

* Take another deep breath in and then slowly exhale. Say: "You are the Light." Imagine people you know covered in brilliant light.

* Take another deep breath in and then slowly exhale. Say: "We are the Light." See your light and everyone else's light coming together.

* Slowly go to a sacred space, a space where you feel safe, full of light and love.

* Call in your spiritual guides. Also, call in one or more person(s) who have achieved great things in this world, someone who is a role model to you. You don't need to have met them.

* Sit down with them and get comfortable.

* Imagine before you the person that you want to be and be with.

* Also, imagine before you the obstacles that prevent these people from manifesting in your life. With the help of your guides and role model, begin to remove the obstacles one by one until this part of your path is clear.

* Now ask your role model, "Where do I need to shift from love to fear?"

* Ask, "What do I have to do?"

* Ask, "Who do I have to be not to live in this fear any longer?"

* Now ask, "What do I need to heal to make this manifest? Where am I not forgiving? What do I have to surrender?"

* Now ask them what the next step is. Be very clear.

* Now step into the miracle. What does it feel like? What does it look like?

* Get in touch with the feelings, the sensations. Use your five senses. Get in the energetic space of how this would feel like.

* When in touch with the sensations, bring them towards you. Imagine your Higher Self gifting it to you.

* Receive this gift, knowing that you are deserving of it.

* Slowly begin to come back your present awareness.

* Breathe three times and with each exhale, say, "There is no order of difficulties in miracles."

Getting clear on what you want seems to be a crucial step in this process, no? Make an inventory of the qualities you would like in your ideal mate. Then start to live these qualities and see what manifests. As you focus on the manifestation piece, don't just focus on the specific outcome but on the feeling of having it. Always keep your behaviors and intentions consistent.

71

Incongruency in this area can lead to some very disastrous results. While you are going through this process, see what areas of your life have been neglected and beef these up somehow.

Now that you have gotten crystal clear on what you desire, it's time to get a whole lot of Namaste and look at your tendencies to hold onto things too tightly. Surrendering outcomes can be a very liberating part of this process. Follow me to the next chapter...

6

SURRENDER OUTCOMES

"Surrender is the faith that the power of love can accomplish anything even when you cannot foresee the outcome."

- Deepak Chopra

One thing that jammed me up in my quest for romance was getting too fixated on specific outcomes. Here I must advise you to have caution and not to get too extreme. While we need to get very clear on what we want, we also can't get too caught up on the specific details. It is not our desire for things that jam us up but our *attachment* to these things that cause misery and pain, as the Buddhists teach.

Let's return to my fixation with Channing Tatum for a minute. Now, as an extreme example, I can get very fixated on being with someone who looks just like Mr. Tatum. I go for the chiseled and hairless abs, dancing ability, light hair and eyes, and the ability to have sex like a porn star. While this is entirely within the realm of possibility, gripping too tightly to this specific outcome can end up in disaster or perpetual singledom.

However, I could go for a guy who is fit. If he has the six-pack abs, great. If not, at least he is fit. I can go for someone who is tall, not someone who specifically is 6'1" like Mr. Tatum. I can go for someone who is a good dancer, not necessarily with the potential to have sex like a porn star (as I envision Mr. Tatum being able to do). I think you get the picture, no?

Miracle Moment:
Surrendering means stop trying to control
what it's going to look like.

For someone like me, it's hard to wrap my head around this notion. While I have often felt empowered by controlling outcomes in the past, it has led to much exhaustion and not to the results I had envisioned. I also missed many opportunities to see what presented itself in the moment. If I obsess about what I want something to look like, I don't see what is in front of me as a better option. It has often been said at Twelve Step meetings, "My best thinking got me here."

Although this example does not pertain to relationships, it does illustrate the point about surrendering outcomes and seeing what is being presented. At the beginning of 2014, I wanted to move into my own practice. I had a vision of what I wanted for my business. I began the search around August of that year. The first place I saw was exactly what I envisioned for my practice. However, the options for leasing were not in my favor. I was distraught because this office space was what I wanted. I looked around, but nothing else appealed to me; it was all vastly different from what I wanted (think Channing Tatum versus Nathan Lane).

As the search continued, I started to lose hope. Suddenly, my brilliant Realtor sent me a picture of a magnificent view of downtown Brooklyn and the East Side of Manhattan. I asked him what the office looked like and we met up. Lo and behold, we not only found what I wanted but something ten times better with the most amazing view. If I had held on too tightly to the specifics of what I wanted, I would have said no to a perfect office space. However, I did hold true to my vision.

Many years ago, while attending a Twelve Step meeting, I recall someone saying something I have never forgotten, about surrender. The speaker, in this case, was talking about the third step ("We made a decision to turn our will and our lives over to the care of God as we understood Him") and she said, "Surrendering for me means that I stop fighting." By controlling and not surrendering, I am fighting against the divine order of the universe and imposing my will over that of God's will.

This type of energy does not attract what we really want, nor does it allow us to be the person we want to be with. Do you want to be with someone who is controlling in his or her every endeavor? This battle can be quite exhausting. Fighting and controlling take up so much energy that can be spent on much more fruitful endeavors.

Another example I can give you about controlling, fighting, and surrendering relates to my journey with my life coach. When I engaged my coach, my goal was to be in this amazing relationship and stop the hamster wheel of emotionally unavailable men in my life. His goal for me was to get completely okay with who I was so I didn't need to be in a relationship. Well, I fought him pretty good on this.

I was like, "I know how to do single. I am okay with it." What I wasn't okay with was who I am. I knew how to be alone but I didn't know how to be single. However, my lack of surrender did not allow me to see this.

A year and change later, after about 10 first dates, three or four second dates, a sixty-nine day relationship, and numerous lovers, I surrendered to what my coach had been telling me all along. Once I surrendered to being okay with who I was, things began to shift on all levels. At the time of this writing, I am single, not really dating, and okay with it. I was finally able to get to this point by surrendering to the need to have to be in a relationship.

Miracle Moment:
I surrender the need to have something
outside of myself make me happy.
I surrender to the wonderful being
that is me, with or without a man.
I stop fighting and start living.

In her book, *A Return to Love*, Marianne Williamson speaks about the divine order of things when talking about surrendering. My favorite example is that an embryo doesn't need anyone to tell it or force it to become a baby. It does so because it is in its programming. An acorn does not need anyone to force it to become a tree. It just does so because of its programming and the laws of the universe. Even things we don't see, like air and gravity, will do their thing without any interference from us. These are universal truths to live by.

My responsibility in all of this is just to show up. I teach my clients to do the work, show up, and surrender outcomes. I can hold on to what it is that I want. I can surrender my outcomes while not controlling and fighting the universe. Not only do I get what I want, but also usually it is something better. My past relationships have taught me that. My relationship with Fernando should have been over long before it subsequently was. However, my need to control outcomes led me to stay in a relationship that had reached its expiration date.

I always like to talk about how I benefitted from a maladaptive behavior such as not surrendering outcomes. Again, let me emphasize that we do need to be specific about what we want and need. However, it's our grasp on the specificity of outcomes that gets us into trouble.

Whenever I got too specific with regards to my romantic partners and held on too tightly with regards to the specificity, I lost out on some pretty fabulous dudes in my past. I recall a few, one in 2004 and another in 2006. Both of these guys were amazing and so loving. However, I deemed one to be "too vanilla" and the other to be "too clingy." They did not fit into my very rigid criteria of my ideal romantic partner.

I did benefit from engaging in this behavior for many reasons. The main one was I did not have to take responsibility for my change and growth and instead pointed the finger at a nasty universe that was conspiring to have me single for the rest of my life. When I encountered a more suitable paramour that did not meet my specifications, I could easily reject him without having to walk through the fears of being vulnerable and possibly falling in love. If you wonder why I would sabotage the very thing I was striving for, think about it for a second: Falling in love requires an intimate level of becoming vulnerable and trusting things could work out. By outright rejecting those suitors that did not meet my specific parameters, I did not have to get to that level of vulnerability.

My biggest lesson in vulnerability came from my friend, Gabby Bernstein. In a lecture, she said, "Shared vulnerability is the greatest expression of love." These words rang true for me the moment she said them and I hold on to the validity this statement has in my life. This book is one of those examples of shared vulnerability. I want you to see what I went through without censorship or over dramatization. I know that through authenticity and vulnerability, I gain a more genuine experience in my relationships.

I will do something a little different this chapter than previous chapters. While I usually love to quote *A Course in Miracles*, now I want to refer to one of the "Four Noble Truths" from Buddhist philosophy. For the sake of reference, I will state the "Four Noble Truths" and speak specifically about the "Second Noble Truth."

1. All existence is suffering.
2. The cause of suffering is craving.
3. The cessation of suffering comes with the cessation of craving.

4. There is a path that leads from suffering.

The Second Noble Truth says it is not our desire for things, but our attachment to those things that causes suffering (or dukkha in Buddhist terms). By surrendering to specific outcomes, I can avoid most suffering. By attaching to specific outcomes, I will create so much personal suffering. A good friend of mine once told me, "Sadness is inevitable, but suffering is an option." I don't know about you guys, but I don't want to suffer if I can avoid it. When I don't surrender outcomes, it's usually because I don't trust in my manifestation abilities or that the universe has my back.

The Teacher's Manual of *A Course in Miracles* says, "Those who are certain of the outcome can afford to wait and wait without anxiety." When I am trying to control outcomes and refuse to surrender, I am not certain of the outcome. I am not trusting in a power greater than myself. I have doubts about what will ultimately happen because I am wanting something too specific and fear that I won't get it. When I surrender outcomes, I can gain a sense of peace and not obsess about the outcome. When I am certain of the outcome (i.e., "I do not believe that I am doomed to be single"), I will manifest what I want.

The day that I surrendered, January 2, 2016, I was at peace. I wrote what I wanted and just let the universe do its thing. Fernando walked in shortly after that. Now, you may say I did not get what I wanted. But if you knew him and compared him to my Manventory, I did get what I want, at least at the time. I didn't walk into that initial meeting with Fernando expecting to meet the man I would fall for. I was walking through life in sync with what was

CASE STUDY

Matt, the Man That Had to Be 180 Pounds

I want to discuss a more unique case I had in my practice. A young man by the name of Matt walked in one day. Matt was a talented and handsome young man trying to find his place in this world (as well as in New York City). Matt was a very fit guy and very talented. However, Matt was plagued with one thing: He was obsessed with packing on muscle and weighing at least 180 pounds. Every time he got on the scale and his weight was less than 180 pounds, he belittled himself. Every time he ate something that was not a muscle-producing food, he belittled himself. Until he got specifically to 180 pounds, he was experiencing a pretty severe dysphoria about himself.

Matt's insistence on the 180 pounds was a way of him controlling what he could not control in his external world (i.e., not being as successful as he thought he should be and not being in a relationship). It was also his maladaptive way of preventing him from changing his ways into more adaptive behaviors. As Matt let go of specific outcomes, he has now liberated himself to enjoy working out for the sake of it as well as releasing his first album and being at peace with being single.

MAKEOVER MOMENT:

Are you ready to drop the rope and stop the tug-of-war you have in your life? Are you ready to surrender? Here are some exercises for you to think about as you go through the process of surrendering outcomes:

1. How do you benefit from being inflexible and holding on to specific outcomes?

2. What is being prevented from happening when you do this?

3. Energetically, how does it feel when you hold on to specific outcomes too rigidly?

4. What do you manifest when you are in this state?

5. What are your fears about surrendering?

6. What could be possible if you would just let it go?

7. How do you benefit from controlling outcomes? How else can you serve this need?

After you have examined surrendering outcomes and relinquishing control, let's take some quiet time to reflect on the following:

"I surrender outcomes."

"I am open to the possibilities the universe provides to me."

"I am certain of my outcomes."

"I don't need to control everything to feel power."

Surrendering outcomes is one of the most difficult steps, in my opinion, for being the person you want to be with. We as human beings want what we want. However, by being too attached to our wants, we may be creating more problems than achieving results. And again, do we want to be a controlling person and/or be with a controlling person? Energetically, how does controlling feel to you? It's not very liberating or attracting, if you ask me. With practice, surrendering becomes almost second nature, and we drop the need to police our lives and the universe.

Have you dropped the need to control yet? Good. The next step of our journey is to recognize "I don't need to be in a relationship (for the reasons I think I do)."

7

I DON'T NEED TO BE IN A RELATIONSHIP
(FOR THE REASONS I THINK I DO)

"It's nice to be with someone but I don't think you need to be in a relationship to feel complete. That would be sad."

- Kristin Davis

This chapter, by far, was the hardest to start and to even think about. Throughout the process of writing this book, while starting each chapter, the universe provided me with very specific lessons to really get me into the content of the chapter. I feared this one because I feared the lessons it would bring.

After my breakup with Fernando, I acted out in various and sundry ways to manage my feelings of hurt and betrayal. You might think that this level of emotional upheaval is crazy since the relationship lasted a whopping sixty-nine days. However, it wasn't so much the actual relationship but what it represented for me.

This relationship represented an opportunity to practice all the skills I had been learning throughout the course of my coaching sessions, as well as in my past relationship history. And in some ways, I thought this relationship was the prize for all the work I had done. While I did fairly well (despite what my ego mind was screaming at me) in my relationship with Fernando, the level of vulnerability I got to in this relationship was so deep—and the subsequent results were somewhat overwhelming—that it is difficult to fathom going through it all again. Despite my apprehension, I know what my heart wants and when a suitable paramour shows up again, I will do the work better and more in alignment with who I am.

I know I am getting to the part in this journey where I will talk about dating. *What if a great guy shows up and I do the work of dating and become vulnerable again? What if I get the same result I got with Fernando? If the new relationship doesn't work out, how will I navigate the pain this time?*

I have experienced some pretty intense fear of being really into a dude and having it not work out. There is an inherent uncertainty in relationships that I have had difficulties dealing with in the past. Being so attached to this relationship for validation and meaning amidst uncertainties is a recipe for panic and dread. I don't know if I want to go through that again.

Fernando and I had made plans to travel and go to Broadway shows. We never got to do any of those things. Yes, I am scared of going through this again. However, as the Course says, "To teach is to learn." So let's start talking about why I/we don't *need* to be in a relationship.

Throughout my relationship history, I have wanted to get into a relationship so I could feel like everyone else, so I could feel normal. However, I don't need to be in a relationship to feel this way.

Miracle Moment:
I don't need to be in a relationship for the reasons I think I need to be.

One distinction I want to make here is the difference between a need and a want. There are some things that we all intrinsically need, basic needs like food, water, shelter, and air. Some are higher-level needs like income or a profession. We also have belonging and self-actualization needs. Abraham Maslow spoke about this in his Theory of Hierarchy of Needs (physiological, safety, belongingness and love, esteem and self-actualization needs). These needs, as postulated by Maslow, are inherently important. However, the degree to which we cling to these needs, as a form of identity and validation is where the problem lies.

The key here is to cultivate the feeling of self-love within our singlehood. Recognizing we are whole, complete, and lacking nothing, whether single or in a relationship, allows our vibrations to attract higher-order people and events in our lives. When I get in the energy of not needing to be in a relationship, I create the space to be in a relationship because it just doesn't hold that tremendous weight it used to or consume so many of my waking moments. I live my life free and clear of any attachments to fear, lack, and all the constraints of my ego mind.

To illustrate this point, think about a time you were in a relationship. Have you ever noticed that you get hit on much more when you are in a relationship than when you are single? That you get hit on more when you are walking free and clear of needing to be in a relationship? Nothing has changed really, except the energy you are putting out there.

How I carry myself in and out of a relationship is really the determining factor, not my relationship status. When I am secure in what I have, I bring more of it—which is why I need to watch myself those times I am in a relationship, as temptation can be very powerful.

With regards to sharing my vulnerabilities, sharing my authentic self equates to a higher-vibe practice. As I mentioned before, Gabby Bernstein said that shared vulnerability is the greatest expression of love. I don't regret having been so vulnerable with Fernando. At times, I do recognize I wasn't authentic. I would approach it coming from the perspective of "Here's 'lil old me;

please don't reject me because of this" versus "This is who I am." His response was one of disdain or apathy. However, when I approached him feeling vulnerable and in a state of authenticity and love, he was more turned on by me. Go figure; my guy gets more turned on by me being authentically vulnerable and not because of my throbbing erection.

As I mentioned earlier, since my breakup with Fernando, I had been acting out. One of those ways has been to troll those lovely dating apps in the hopes of numbing the feelings of hurt and loss or banging some dude(s) for validation. While quite successful in doing so, it was transient and left me still wanting something more meaningful like I thought I had with Fernando.

I remember feeling a sense of desperation to replace him with someone else soon after our breakup. Not so much because I wanted to be in a relationship, but because I felt I had screwed up. A new relationship would allow me the opportunity to undo the mistakes I'd made or run away from them somehow. When I was in this state of mind, I kept attracting guys who were just like Fernando in scary ways. Once my desperation diminished, I started attracting much more suitable men and none of them was anything like Fernando.

I decided it was time to give the apps a bit of a break and I went on a self-imposed hiatus. What I found out was that being alone wasn't so bad. Sure, the loneliness (and horniness) would creep in, but for the most part, I found spending time by myself wasn't so bad. I had time to fill that void with things I enjoyed doing. I became obsessed with making knotted mala beads.

During this hiatus, I was also able to deal with the feelings I had been stuffing with men and alcohol. At the end of this app hiatus, I was able to not only embrace my singledom, but also heal some of the hurt from Fernando. I wondered, though: *How do I start to cultivate this newfound appreciation for being single and, at the same time, stay high vibe enough to attract a worthy suitor?*

I think that for myself and many others that I have known, relationships are a way of feeling connected in a disconnected world. In this Internet age, we don't send snail mail or call someone or meet someone in a social setting. We sit on our smart devices and try to make connections there, romantic and otherwise. I don't need to be in a relationship to feel connected. When I thought I was getting a connection, I was left feeling more disconnected than I had previously. Relationships only temporarily ease the sense of separation if the sole foundation of the relationship is to have someone there and feel connected.

I remember Gabby mentioning in a lecture that we need to add more friendships into our romance and more romance into our friendships. What I took this to mean was that I needed to honor a romantic relationship as just as important as a friendship. I need to have a solid friendship with my significant other and not to let the relationship be the end all, be all of my life, which is a concept previously discussed in Chapter Two. If I make the romantic relationship into a solid friendship, I can reinforce that I don't need to be in a relationship.

I also thought to myself that I had had an easier time losing a friend than I did losing a romantic partner. While the two relationships are different, I need to value both relationships as equally important as to not have the romantic relationship be the focal point of my existence. This led to a greater appreciation and gratitude for the friends I do have, particularly those who carried me after the breakup with Fernando.

Believing I needed to be in a relationship to feel normal was a way to avoid the internal work that I continually have to do. Getting ready for most things, especially a romantic relationship, requires an inner search into those areas I don't like to look at and face the demons I cover up through avoidance and/or self-medication. One of the issues I continually cover with clients is the need to stop looking externally to make the internal better.

Whenever I seek anything outside myself to "fix" me, I perceive only the lack in my life. By focusing and being grateful for the abundance internally, I attract more abundance and rely less on external factors to cure what ails me. Many, if not all, Twelve Step programs were formed to help people move from an external "locus of control" to an internal one. The whole notion of "locus of control" comes from personality psychology, which speaks to one's ability to believe they have control over the outcome of their lives, as opposed to external factors beyond their control.

Shifting from an external locus of control to an internal locus of control is one of the best ways to shift the mindset from needing to be in a relationship to not needing to be in a relationship. This does not eliminate the want of being in a relationship. What I am suggesting here is to change to a higher-vibe frequency to attract more appropriate suitors, rather than just look for anyone to fill a void and make us feel normal and/or connected.

A Course In Miracles says the separation essentially is a detour into fear: "The separation introduced the idea of lack to you. Lack is untruth or illusion. Believing in illusion is a choice and it will disappear in an instant if you want it to because it is only a misperception." We are not lacking by being single. Being in a relationship will not cure the sense of separation that may exist. The work entails knowing we are okay single and that a relationship only complements our lives. It does not define our lives or our worth as a person.

CASE STUDY

Patrick, the Man Who Needed to Be in a Relationship

I have been working with a client, Patrick, who seemed to perseverate on being in a relationship. Patrick was born and raised in the Midwest in a conservative family. Patrick struggled with his sexual orientation as a gay man for most of his life, despite having a rather supportive family. He looked at his peers and wanted what they had but felt that by being gay, he could not.

Once Patrick moved to New York City, he felt more liberated to explore his sexual orientation. However, because he did not meet the stereotypical pattern of a gay male, he felt more isolated than he did in the Midwest. He did not have the stereotypical gay male body or any of the other stereotypes consistent with gay men. Patrick kept comparing himself, this time to his gay peers. He became desperate to be in a relationship to feel a sense of belonging and self-worth as well as feeling less separated. Patrick wanted to be like everyone else. However, his journey led to more of what he was trying to avoid because he was seeking a relationship for all the wrong reasons. Many dates turned into disasters.

My work with Patrick dealt with not only not making relationships his Higher Power but also to know he did not need to be in a relationship for the reasons he thought he did. This was a hard concept for him to grasp, as he continued to need to be in a relationship as opposed to wanting to be in a relationship. He was able to let go of his need to be in a relationship as holding on to this need was making him miserable. Patrick had hit rock bottom emotionally and was trying to see things differently. While he is presently not in a relationship, he is well on his way to recognizing more of his self-worth as single gay man, not needing to be in a relationship to define him.

MAKEOVER MOMENT:

So, let's take a personal journey on not needing to be in a relationship for the reasons you think you do. These questions are geared towards turning your work more inward than outward. This creates space for that special someone to come in. Bring your journal out and answer the following questions:

1. How does it feel energetically when you are "needing" instead of "wanting" to be in a relationship?

2. What kind of partners do you attract when you are in this energetic state?

3. Are you scared of being vulnerable in a relationship and how has this had a negative impact on your past relationships and current potential dating/relationships?

4. Have you acted out in ways that are not in alignment with your highest self and what were you trying to avoid in doing so?

5. What are the benefits of facing our demons head on without the use of external sources of validation/numbing?

6. How does a need versus a want feel energetically for you?

7. How can you cultivate more of an internal locus of control with regards to your life circumstances and your relationships?

8. What areas of your life are you avoiding looking at?

9. Where is your locus of control?

10. How do you distinguish between a want and a need?

11. How can you powerfully share your vulnerabilities with another person?

12. How can you cultivate feelings of appreciation for your single status?

13. How can you talk yourself off the ledge when the uncertainty of a relationship invades your thinking?

I know this was a rough one, but so worth it in the long run. Treat yourself to some self-care moments and ponder on the following affirmations:

"I don't need to be in a relationship for the reasons I think I do."

"My externals do not control my internal state."

"I am high vibe when I am authentic and vulnerable."

"I look at all areas of my life with courage."

"I am present to what is in front of me."

I hope you now see why you don't need to be in a relationship for the reasons you think you do. The determining factor here is to recognize that relationships are less of a need and more of a want. We all want to belong, and having that special someone certainly does fulfill that. However, when the reason for our existence is that relationship, we slip into a lower-vibe energy and we become the person we don't ever want to be with (unless you suffer from Narcissistic Personality Disorder). Shifting our happiness to more of an internal job than something reliant on external factors changes our ability in a positive way to get the things we want in life.

After doing all this work, you're probably wondering, Are we ever going to get to that first date? Well, there is one more step before we get there—so let me ask you:

Are you here yet?

8

#AREYOUHEREYET?

"Your task is not to seek for love, but merely to seek and find all the barriers within yourself that you have built against it."

- A Course in Miracles

So, you are probably wondering, When do I get to go on a date? Before you can go on a date, you must complete one final step: *Are you here yet?*

Often in our quest for love, we forget the most important person in the equation: ourselves. We look externally for something to make us complete. That is why the first chapters of this book are all about you and getting yourself ready for relationships. How many times have we said or heard our friends say, "No matter what I do, I keep attracting the same crap?"

Well, here is the question to ask: What's the common denominator? The good and bad news is: You are the common denominator in all your relationships. Have you done the work to be the best possible version of yourself you can be at any given moment? This will create the space for that right person to come in because you are the right person.

Miracle Moment:
*The most important relationship we
can ever have is with ourselves.*

Who we are as individuals is the strongest foundation we can ever build. If we do not have a solid foundation, whatever we build on top of it will not be steady or well fortified. This is true of any structure. It needs to have a solid foundation, as well as pillars to hold it together. That is not to say that there don't come continual points in our lives that would require us to look at ourselves and fix a small crack in our foundation and/or pillars.

The work of self is a lifelong process. However, the work of making oneself available for a relationship can pause when we feel we are there. By doing the work from the preceding chapters, you may very well see that the relationship you are yearning for isn't as important as being comfortable with who you are. I know that this has been the case for me.

Our current society is looking outside of itself for happiness: "I will be happy when..." As a former cigarette smoker, I remember saying every semester in grad school, "I will quit smoking after finals." Finals came and I never quit smoking. I did so when I said it was enough and I wanted to show up differently in my own life. One of the things I regularly work on with my clients is the whole epidemic of "I'll be happy when..." Happiness is something we can choose at any given point, regardless of present circumstances. Why wait to be happy? BE HAPPY NOW.

And here is the other funny thing: While that thing or event you are hoping for will give you the happiness you seek for a short period, it does not provide a long-lasting solution to the problem. It's like taking a painkiller for a brain tumor. You have to treat what's going on inside before you worry about the outside. The moment you do that, external gratification loses some of its appeal. Internal gratification, while appearing to take longer to come about, always provides a consistent and more permanent happiness and power than that external event/thing.

While on the subject of gratification, have you ever noticed we have absolutely no patience for the things we want out of life? Whether it's a fitness goal or a relationship, we want it now, and we want it fast. This feeds into a lack mentality, as well as fear mentality. We fear if we don't have something or gain something instantly, it's not worth the work.

Miracle Moment:
The work is always worth it.
It is the process that provides the
happiness and not necessarily the
result. They work hand in hand.

Being in the process cultivates a state of being that is very powerful and lends more into an abundance mentality. Think of a time you rushed into something only because it looked good "on paper," and you wanted it so badly. How did it work out for you? Probably not great. This chapter is an opportunity for you to get yourself as ready as you can for that date, and possibly that relationship.

Many mental health professionals and life coaches will tell you your external experience is largely based on your internal state. Look at your very own day-to-day experiences. Notice the times in which you see something one way, but a change in your mood will change your perspective on that very same thing. Herein lies the miracle answer to getting okay with who you are. Make sure you work on your internal states and stop worrying so much about how the outside looks. This will make getting okay with yourself so much easier and pave the way for that love to come your way.

We don't see things how they are; we see things how we are. Take your favorite movie or television show. While you may think this is the best you have ever seen, ask any number of people and you will get a different opinion on the very same thing. Why? Everyone has their sense of objectivity over the same thing, and this then creates different perspectives.

I would like to add one of my favorite and most thought-provoking lines from *A Course in Miracles*: "Your task is not to seek for love, but merely to seek and find all the barriers within yourself that you have built against it." All I ever want is right here, right now. I just have to remove all of the self-imposed blocks that prevent me from accessing it.

The major block for me has been feeling that being in a relationship would make me feel normal or would make me like everyone else. The funny thing is that, for the most part, people in relationships aren't always okay with who they are. Their motivation for being in a relationship is to fill that perceived void within themselves.

Here's a challenging thought: *What if there is no void?* It doesn't exist. It is a byproduct of our fear-based ego mind or societal pressures or any myriad of things. What we think is a void is blocking our access to our true power. Where those blocks come from really doesn't matter. You have them now. Your job is to remove those blocks. I am not saying that getting to the source of the blocks isn't important, but it is not paramount to get to the point that you start to remove your obstacles. Removing these obstacles allows us to step powerfully into our own lives.

As I have done in all the previous chapters, I like to talk about how I have benefitted from this way of being. As I write this, I recall all the ways that I have been there for myself and have found much success. I have an amazing business working with the most inspirational clients. My work with clients keeps me working on myself. I have the best friends and support system that a person can ask for. I am in good health and look great for someone my age. I completed a doctorate while working full time. I relocated my entire life from Miami to Brooklyn almost seamlessly. For the most part, I faced my fears and inner demons to create space for these amazing things to happen. I continue to do the work, no matter what.

Something else will show up for me to continue to grow. I enter into these new experiences with eagerness, albeit with some fear as well. I look upon the person I am today and see that I have come a long way. All these things have been a success because I showed up for myself, and by doing so, showed up for others. In the area of relationships, however, I have not really shown up for myself.

By staying in the problem of "not being here yet," I avoid responsibility for having to take charge of my own life and get to point the finger at others. Anytime I stay in the problem, it allows me to do just that, stay in the problem. The solution can be quite simple in theory but difficult in execution. This always reminds me of something Marianne Williamson says: "It is difficult not because it is hard but because it is different."

When I first started working with my coach, my goal was to have a life and a loving relationship just like his. However, his goal for me was quite different, which was for me to be "wildly okay" with who I am. I never really got that idea and kept the undercurrent of my work with him to be getting that relationship. Then it happened. Then it was gone. Then I was crazy for many months running from my sense of loneliness and failure.

I eventually came to my senses, having hit another emotional bottom after months of craziness, and saw what I needed to do. I had to up my game and get clear on why. I would not trade all the craziness I participated in for anything in the world as today I feel very strongly that I can answer the question, "Am I here yet?" *Yes, I am.*

When we are in the state of being there for ourselves, so many doors and opportunities become available. There is a wonderful lesson (#35) in *A Course in Miracles* that says, "There is nothing my holiness cannot do." As you read through the lesson, it speaks about our inherent greatness and how by recognizing this greatness that is within all of us, a power greater than ourselves is made available to us. There is nothing we can't manifest.

What this passage tells me is very important. When I am in my power, when I am here for myself—my holiness—there is nothing I can't do. We all have that inner power we forget to connect with. We become so focused on having all the external circumstances being just right that we don't go within and burst through whatever blocks we are experiencing. Spiritual practices have been teaching the masses that the answers are "going within" and being in the present moment. This is my main go-to for when I need to show up powerfully in my life and manifest the crap of what I want to create.

So, usually this is the time in which I share with you an experience with a client to illustrate what I have been talking about in the current chapter. For the purpose of this chapter, I will deviate from that pattern and the client in question will be me.

As I mentioned earlier, when I initially started my personal work with my coach, my goal was to be in a relationship. His goal was for me to get okay with the idea that the relationship was not so much of a need but a want. I was not with this philosophy but, like a new person in Alcoholics Anonymous working with his sponsor, I wanted what he had, so I did what he suggested. I did a lot of the work I outlined in the previous chapters, but again, the motivation for doing the work was for that relationship and not to be okay with *myself*, as my coach had suggested.

Along came Fernando and you know how that ended. In the process of writing this book, it became important for me to live the philosophies I was discussing here for authenticity purposes. On the original outline, this chapter was the dating chapter. However, I spent two months without writing a single word on the dating chapter out of fear. I had done all this work, and now I had to put this stuff into practice. *What if I am full of crap? What if everything I say doesn't work?* I was paralyzed with these fear-based thoughts and could not write at all.

At the end of November 2016, I was working with my mentor, Gabby Bernstein and her team of coaches for the Spirit Junkie Masterclass Level 2. On this fateful day, Gabby was talking about book writing. She had us pair up, and I was with my fellow coach, Alyssa. We were chatting about our books in progress, and we came up with thought-provoking subtitles. This was monumental for me, as the subtitle for this book, "Being the person you want to be with," not only tied my book together more coherently; it also sparked a conversation about what the next chapter should be.

Alyssa and I chatted about how we forget ourselves in the process of dating and relationships. She then said, "Do the soul work you need to do so that you would date you." Through the process of working with Alyssa, the blocks suddenly lifted. The next step in this work wasn't necessarily a date but for me to be okay with who I am and the work I had done and continue to do. I had to ask myself the question: *Am I here yet?*

It was the last step I needed to undertake for everything from the previous chapters to come together. I needed to look at how comfortable I was with myself and what areas still needed work.

A Course in Miracles says, "Only what you are not giving can be lacking in any situation." When I perceive lack in my internal and external world, I have to look at what I am not giving to the "lacking situation." With regards to relationships, what I was not giving was being totally and profoundly okay with who I am. I finally got it.

The work of the previous chapters was vital, but it all came together when I asked myself the question, "Am I here yet?" That was what was lacking. I wasn't the person I wanted to be with. I kept looking for that external validation or sources of gratification to come and fix me. There is nothing to fix because I know today that I am whole and complete. My wish for you, my dear readers, is for you to recognize your greatness and completeness.

MAKEOVER MOMENT:

The time has come when we will be dating. Before we do that, we need to answer a few questions...

1. In what areas are you not showing up for your own life?

2. In what areas have you consistently shown up in your life and created miracles?

3. Look back on your life and see what you have been able to create. What was your internal state at the time that facilitated these creations to be made manifest?

4. What are the conditions in which you rely on external circumstances to be a certain way for you to do something?

5. What can you affirm to be true for you so you can access your internal power and burst through the blocks?

6. How do you tap into your inner power?

7. How can you be happy now?

8. Would you date you?

9. What obstacles have you imposed on yourself that prevent you from accessing the love that resides within you?

10. Are you here yet?

Wow, this was an intense journey, no? Take the opportunity to relax for a bit and affirm what you know to be true for you. Sit with these meditative affirmations (and refine them to make them more you) and get ready.

"There is no void."

"I release all the obstacles to accessing the love that resides within."

"I would date me."

"I can be happy now no matter what."

"Love does not need to be rushed."

Continue to can create a list of affirmations that resonate with you and allow you to answer the question, "Am I Here Yet?"

So, there you have it. We have made peace with our past. We have gotten totally okay with who we are. We have recognized our inner power. Finally, are at the point where we can say whether we are here for ourselves.

Does this make us ready to finally go on a date? The answer is YES. Now, let's look at "You ...On a Date."

9

YOU...ON A DATE

"I enjoy dating. I love first dates. I think they are incredibly fascinating studies in human psychology. When you sit across someone on a first date and things are going all right, you talk objectives. We want to win each other over, so how do you win someone over? You have to put the best foot forward."

- Chris Pine

I remember when I first thought I was ready to date. I dove in with full force. I *thought* I was ready and over Fernando. I had been doing the work with my coach. I *thought* I had done the work I had outlined in the previous chapters. *It was time.* What ended up happening was one disastrous first date after another. You have heard some of the stories, but I think it's time to share the worst first date in human history.

I met this guy on Scruff and made plans for a date, not just meaningless sex, as this was what he presented as we chatted. He asked me to meet him at a local bar. When I got there, he wasn't. I waited around for thirty minutes and called him. He was getting his hair cut about two miles away and asked that I meet him there. However, he didn't give me an exact address, and it took me another thirty minutes to get there and find the place.

We finally met, and he planted a kiss on me—which I thought was a good sign—and we walked to a local bar. He ordered drinks for us and went to the bathroom because he wasn't happy with his haircut and wanted to fix it in the mirror. I waited around for about another seven minutes, and he came back with a "friend." When he tried to introduce me to said friend, he stumbled when remembering his name (*hello, red flag*).

I came to find out he had just received fellatio from this dude he had met in the bathroom. The dude was waiting for his drug dealer to bring him some cocaine, which my date seemed very interested in receiving. I chugged my drink and left after a few other embarrassing moments that I can't fathom disclosing in public.

Looking back, I see I was still in the space of needing to be in a relationship versus wanting to be in a relationship. Sometimes things have to get worse before they get better. When I am in a space of not knowing what I want to manifest, the universe conspires in my favor and gives me one learning experience after another. I will continue to have this experience presented to me until I learn the lesson. When we are in the space of not getting clear on what you want, we will attract disasters like Mr. Bathroom Fellatio. I'll share a few more lessons from this disaster of a first date ...

You "meet" someone by whatever medium, set up that first date, and here come the obsessive thoughts. You have planned your wedding before you have even met. While you are on the first date, you jump to thoughts of what the future holds and will you kiss or have coitus or any number of anxiety-producing thoughts that knock you out of the present moment and stop you from being fully in the experience. You have met, fallen in love, had children, bought a house, and gotten divorced before you even arrive at your first date.

So, you on a date. What's the first thing that you need to do? Remember one thing: YOU HAVE NOTHING TO LOSE (unless you have an experience like I had where this dude and I went out to dinner, agreed to split the check, and his credit card got denied and I lost thirty dollars). You are just two people getting to know each other. Be present. Be in the moment. Be open to the learning experience because in one way or another, this date has presented itself for a reason and that reason is to learn. Remember, every relationship is an assignment. Ask yourself, "What's my curriculum here?"

Think of it like a job interview for the person with whom you are on a date. This person is applying for a position in your life (insert missionary position joke here). Instead of taking the stance of "Oh my God, is he going to want me? Is it going to work out?" think to yourself that you are *essentially interviewing someone to be a part of your life in some capacity.* That capacity can be as a friend, or romantic partner, or even an amazing learning experience. I also suggest you know what you want for this position before you agree on the date. If you don't know the "job qualifications" for the position, you will just get anyone who is willing to apply, not necessarily the right person for the job.

Each interaction with this person tells you if they are a right "fit" for your company (figuratively speaking, of course). Having this mentality will allow for the pressure to come right off and allow you to be more present when you are on the date. You can even go so far as to have a verbal warning, first write-up, and termination after second write-up (of course, I wouldn't actually write it up and give it to them).

As an older gay man, sometimes I would go on dates with eligible dudes only because they were okay with being with an older man and were moderately attractive. Of course, I got the disasters or learning experiences that I got. I wasn't screening and interviewing based on job qualifications, but on the basis that they wanted to be with me. Address your stigmas before entering into the dating pool (more on that in a bit). Go over your Manventory and see if this individual meets that list (at least to some degree, for God's sake).

Get to know who this person is before making them your future ex-boyfriend (or ex-girlfriend). Your feelings can be a gauge on how this person fits your needs. I am not referring to the anxiety-producing thoughts of what will happen. I am referring to be present to how you feel around this person.

I have had dates where I couldn't get a word in edgewise. I have had dates where I felt I needed to be someone other than I was due to fear, whether caused by my ego mind or something the other person was doing or being. And I have also had first dates where I felt I could be authentically me. I can talk about all my loves and hobbies, feel like I am heard, and reciprocate that sentiment when my date is talking. This is my goal for relationships: to be in a loving and mutually reciprocal relationship.

This calls for a true connection to our inner power. Nothing shakes us to our core more than relationships. Volumes of books and thousands of songs revolve around love and relationships (didn't Taylor Swift make it big after she wrote an album following a breakup?). If you have done the work outlined in the preceding chapters, you will be able to stand in your inherent power while you are on a date. This way, regardless of the results, you will know you did your best. Dates can be scary, especially if they don't work out despite you wanting them to work out.

Let's talk about rejection for a second. Rejection can feel quite devastating (except for when I didn't get a call back from Mr. Bathroom Fellatio guy). Rejection can feel so personal. However, often, rejection has nothing to do with you. Even with Mr. Bathroom Fellatio guy, some other dudes would have been totally into the scenario that was unfolding that night.

Miracle Moment:
Rejection is not about rejecting you.
Rejection is the other person saying no
to the notion of you and them together.

Rejection was one of those things that stifled my ability to date, or better yet, I allowed it to stifle my ability to date. With every rejection, I was devastated. I took it to mean that there was something inherently wrong with me. After some rejection throughout my dating experience, I created a story—actually, several stories—that I wasn't attractive enough, or I wasn't muscular enough, or my schlong wasn't big enough, etc. The stories I created due to taking rejection so personally was that essentially *I wasn't enough*.

Throughout my personal development, particularly in recent years, I know that *I am enough*. Many times, after a rejection, I would hear about this dude through the grapevine and see he actually did me a favor and I dodged a bullet. However, while I stayed in the story of I wasn't enough, I could not date due to self-preservation, and once again, blame everyone else and not take responsibility for my own life. This is how I benefited from staying in this story. It illustrates the connection to how we benefit from any maladaptive way of thinking and/or being: "I don't have to take responsibility for my own life and blame everyone else for it and feel safe." After Fernando, I was tired of feeling safe. It was time to open the gates.

Here is also an excellent opportunity to address an issue that is very prevalent in the gay community: stigmas. Many of the gay men I have worked with in my practice face any number of stigmas in our community. The nature of the topics varies from body image to sexual practices to HIV status. Regardless of the stigma, the most important thing to address is self-stigma. I can have all the approval and validation from the entire world, but if I don't feel it for myself, it won't matter.

We have seen this with celebrities. They have the adoration of millions, yet they destroy their lives through drugs, alcohol, or not taking care of their mental health. Stigma begins and ends with me. Check your stigmas at the door when you start dating.

Addressing and overcoming your self-stigmas is so important. If I walk around with a scarlet letter of a stigma, scared of rejection, guess what? That is what I will attract in my life. I will continually attract men who will reject me for said stigma. However, if I work through my stigma and know who I am in the context of my essential self, while I may encounter dudes who will reject me, the chances are greater that I will not attract those men.

CASE STUDY

Anthony, the Man Who Lived in Self-Stigma

I was working with a client named Anthony, an older gay male who was diagnosed with HIV several years ago. Anthony was a professional at the top of his field; however, he had a secret life as very few people knew about his HIV status. He was rejected, in quite an ugly way, shortly after his diagnosis, and since then, he didn't date much. He would have the occasional hook-up without disclosing his HIV status (he was undetectable at the time) and would occasionally resort to hiring escorts. After a few years of this behavior, this started to not sit well with him and he sought professional help.

Anthony didn't know where to begin in therapy. He still carried so much shame about his HIV status that he didn't want to date. After some time doing some self-love and reframing work, I encouraged Anthony to start dating. Since he still held on to the notion that guys would reject him because of his HIV status, which was what he kept attracting. So, we paused on the dating and got to work on his self-perception and working through his self-stigmas. It took a little bit but he got through the discomfort of disclosing his status, and while he did encounter the occasional rejection, he was actually met with less rejection than before and he got to the point where it didn't bother him anywhere near as much as it used to.

I want to spend a brief moment on the notion of where to meet a potential significant other. Many people say you can't meet quality people at a club or on an app, but I say they're wrong. You can meet quality people just about anywhere. Don't focus on the where so much, but focus rather on the work you need to do with yourself to lay the groundwork for that special someone to come in.

Another thing that my ego still struggles with is the thoughts of, *Well, it's his turn to call/text* or *I am not going to make the first move.* If the fit is right, be you and do what you would want the other person to do. Don't be clingy about it, but don't keep a scorecard either. Nothing will ruin the experience more than keeping score. And finally, if he doesn't call back or text at the speed you would want him to, relax. People react to things in such different ways. I usually can't call/text back right away due to the nature of my job and I let folks know that from the get go. There is likely an alternate explanation why he hasn't returned your text/call within 2.5 seconds.

The Course basically says we only have one problem: Our thoughts of separation. Lesson #80 from *A Course in Miracles* says: "Let me recognize my problems have been solved. If you are willing to recognize your problems, you will recognize that you have no problems." Let's expand on this.

Separation is the enemy of all relationships: family, friendships, and romantic. We think we are separate from others, either in a narcissistic way or low self-esteem way. Essentially, two types of separation occur here. We separate ourselves from our true selves. This is the self that lives in integrity, power, and authenticity. This is the self that has accomplished and is capable of great things. The other separation believes that someone outside of ourselves will complete us, is better than us, and can make us whole. Once we connect to that higher self, squash the thoughts of separation, and recognize our connection with others, the problem is solved.

To further elaborate on this concept, let's look at something. While dating, you can recognize the problem has been solved by not focusing so much on whether it is a date or not. The point here is not to focus on the date and/or the outcome. The issue is knowing the universe has your back and will provide you with the right person for the right learning experience. Whether this experience is Mr. Bathroom Fellatio guy or the man you will marry, it doesn't matter. Take a step back and look for the lesson. All you need to do is show up and show up powerfully and authentically. No pressure now, right?

MAKEOVER MOMENT:

Wow, that was an exhausting first date, no? I never promised this work would be easy. I'd like to think it would give you different results than what you are used to. Let's look at some of the things you can work on for you on a date:

1. What are some of the things that knock you out of the present moment?

2. How can you create more awareness of when you are not in the present moment?

3. What are some ways in which you can recalibrate yourself so that you are fully present?

4. Look at your Manventory. Get really clear on what it is that you want prior to going out on a date. This way you will know if this is a good candidate for the job or not.

5. How do you view rejection and how can you reframe this belief if it is holding you back from being your fabulous self?

6. How can you sense thoughts of separation from others and move towards a place of unity?

7. What has been the learning experience of your past relationships/dating experiences?

8. How can you reframe perceived problems as l earning experiences?

Affirm your truth with these statements:

"There are no problems. Just learning experiences."

"I have nothing to lose."

"Rejection has nothing to do with me."

"I live stigma free."

"I am present in all my endeavors."

Changing the mental framework in which we perceive dates as well as others and ourselves will lead to changes in your dating experience. Fear of rejection may lead you straight into paralysis if you don't do the reframing. When you are dating, you have nothing to lose. Be yourself. You are so amazing so let that date of yours experience how amazing you are!

When a dating experience is successful, it will likely lead to a relationship. Let's move on to the next phase of this journey and talk about relationships ...

10

SO, YOU'RE IN A
RELATIONSHIP NOW

"Whether I am single or in a relationship, I'm the same person. The same human being."

- William Levy

Welcome. You are now in a relationship. You're thinking, *So what do I do now?*

Well, how the fuck do I know? Have you not been paying attention to my rather tragic relationship history? This book has never been about getting the relationship. This book has been about being the person you want to be with regardless of your relationship status. Hence the subtitle.

For the thirty-six hours I was officially in the relationship with Fernando (I say "officially" because that's the period that he allowed me the title of boyfriend), I thought I had arrived. Everything I had been doing in my personal work had led to the moment where:

I could change my relationship status on Facebook (I was asked not to do so, by the way).

I could finally say, "Oh, my boyfriend and I ..."

I could finally do all those things that I had been longing for and say all the things that coupled people say.

Sadly, because of my fixation on being in a relationship, I focused more on him than I did on me. Being in a relationship is much more than just changing your relationship status on social media or talking about what you and your boyfriend did over the weekend. This was the phase in my development in which I had to do the most work.

Miracle Moment:
*Surrendering means stop trying
to control what it's going to look like.*

When we are in relationships, the work doesn't stop. On the contrary, the work continues, and we have to up our vigilance game. We have to be conscious of our self-care so that we can maintain our integrity in the relationship we are in. Being the person we want to be with does *not* stop just because we are with the person we want to be with.

We do all this work, read all these books, attend all these seminars to get that relationship. Then when we are in it, we lose sight of who we are. In the beginning of my courtship with Fernando, I noticed some red flags. However, they appeared not to be insurmountable, so I continued the courtship. These red flags led to my detour into intense fear and losing myself for the better of 60 days. My whole focus was on getting into and staying in this relationship that would have made me normal and would have solved all my problems. Nothing could have been further from the truth, and it had little to do with him.

Once I received the title of boyfriend, I was happy. This was it. I had done the work and gotten the result. When the title was taken away, I did everything in my power to regain it. I never spoke up for my own needs for the remainder of the relationship. I didn't want to rock the boat in case I lost him "again." I let him take control of the relationship because I knew for sure this would be the way to get him to give me a relationship status again, this time more permanently. There was even a request made by him that went against everything I believe to be true for me, that I almost considered compromising. *I stopped being his "boyfriend" and essentially became his bitch.*

The whole topic of red flags can be a tricky one to speak about in a book, as red flags are usually quite individual and vary from person to person. What we need to do is to notice when something comes up in the relationship, and be brutally honest with ourselves about whether we can live with it or not. But be truthful about it, folks. We are strong enough to advocate for ourselves when something comes up that doesn't feel right. Honesty and communication are key here.

Make an honest appraisal of whether this is a red flag that you need to address or if it's something you can live with. There is no need to shrink in the face of adversity just to not upset our partner. It is important for them to address their red flags about us. They and we may not have the insight that this is concerning for the relationship.

Holding on to these things create an undercurrent of resentment as well as scorecards (more on this in a bit). I remember how much this has happened to so many of my clients over the years. This brings to mind something I work on with all of my clients—and sadly, something I did not practice myself in most of my major relationships—and that is making compromises and compromising yourself.

I am a person who can get pretty stuck in his ways. Making compromises is something I have to be very vigilant about. I remember giving Fernando a hard time because I wanted to see this comic book–related movie and he didn't want to see it because he wasn't familiar with the franchise. I struggled with this and got to the realization that it was not a big deal that he didn't want to see this movie. He is not the comic book junkie that I am. This does not say anything about him or me. This is just what it is. I could and did make a compromise. We settled into our evening watching a musical-type movie, something we both could get enjoy. Now, this is making compromises.

I always say my future husband will likely be a sports enthusiast, something that could drive me to suicide. However, if he wanted me to watch the Super Bowl with him, it's no big deal. However, Homeboy will have to watch the Tony Awards or the latest movie of the *X-Men* franchise. We do things for our partners that they want and also that don't compromise who we are as a person, and vice versa. It's not a big deal that I don't get to see (insert comic book movie name) on opening weekend.

Now, something I have not been very good at is avoiding compromising myself. In all three of my major relationships, I made the mistake of doing so. Since I had always made relationships my Higher Power, I would do everything in my power to stay in the relationship, even if it meant compromising my being. With Mick, I gave up my friends because they did not approve of who he had become. With Dean, I didn't speak up when I had to. With Fernando, well, I did a mixture of both and then some to stay in the relationship.

The person who will ultimately end up with us—and those along the way that don't stick around for whatever reason—will love us for who we are. There is nothing sexier and more attractive than someone who stands in their power and doesn't compromise who they are. Compromising oneself for the sake of staying in a relationship is a prescription for disaster.

This goes back to the concept of wanting to belong and wanting to be like everyone else. We have this misguided perception that a relationship defines us, defines our success, and defines our normality. No relationship, even one with Channing Tatum, is worth any one of us compromising who we are. While making compromises is fine, saying no to who you essentially are isn't. I am very big on spirituality, and my practices help me be the best version of me I can be (refer to the Appendix for suggestions on self-care practices). I would love to be with someone who does the same, but I can also be just as happy with someone who is open to my spiritual practices and maybe has some of his own. That is a compromise that does not compromise who I am. I think that if we practice this main idea in our relationships, we have a formula for success.

I also want to bring up the subject of scorecards again. It's easy to keep score of what your partner does or doesn't do. I challenge you to turn the scorecard on yourself and see where you are not the person you want to be, as well as the person you want to be with. Most times, as my teaching partner John says, relationships hold a mirror up to us. They show us an unrecognized part of ourselves that we need to face.

Miracle Moment:
If I feel that my partner is withholding love,
I need to see where I am withholding love.

If I want something special for Valentine's Day, I need to speak up and ask and plan. Our partners are not mind readers. We need to ask for what we want and not sit there seething in resentment because they didn't guess we wanted to see the latest X-Men movie on opening night.

How I benefitted from this problem is difficult to identify. *Why would I continually compromise myself to stay in a relationship?* The very question just provided the answer. Since being in the relationship was my everything, I didn't have a problem compromising everything to maintain the relationship. Once I got the man, I wanted to keep him, even if it meant losing myself in the process.

This is the perfect place to talk about what the Course refers to as a "special relationship" and a "holy relationship." A special relationship is one in which we project onto another person the notion of lack and make them the external thing that will cure us of that lack. This is why I dislike the label "my other half." I'm sorry, but if your relationship is your other half, then there is something not quite right with the way you perceive yourself. By perceiving ourselves as lacking something and then latching onto another person to fill that void, we are taking from them and not giving anything to the relationship.

When we are in a special relationship, we walk around with a perceived void in the very fabric of our existence. And no matter how much your partner is giving you, it will never be enough, as we need to be filling that void. We need to know there is no void. In my special relationship with Fernando, I essentially was holding him hostage. I was making him my everything because I wasn't doing it for myself at the time.

Now, a holy relationship is a whole other matter. A holy relationship is when we shift our perception from one of lack to one of wholeness. When I recognize there is nothing lacking about who I am and that another person does not complete me (insert Dr. Evil quote here), I am in a holy relationship. The notion of separation does not exist in a holy relationship. We are two complete individuals who are together to spread love in the world, not to fulfill some perceived lack for the other person.

When taking all of this into consideration, I think that the basic perception to incorporate when we are in a relationship is that a relationship complements our lives. While it can certainly add to our lives, it's not the only thing that holds meaning.

CASE STUDY

Colin, the Man Who Compromised Himself
to Stay in the Relationship

Colin came to me seeking the assistance of a Latino therapist to help him deal with a long-distance relationship he was having with a Latino man (Colin is not Latino himself). While traveling, Colin met this tall drink of Latin water that rocked his world. Sadly, this same drink of water lived in a country that did not allow him to make a lot of money.

This man wooed Colin into a long-distance relationship. He seemed to say all the right things and eventually got Colin to start supporting him financially. Colin was so smitten by him (and was hot off a breakup) that he started supporting his then boyfriend.

Colin felt this man gave him everything that his last relationship hadn't given him. He figured it wasn't such a big deal to support his new man, as long as he was getting what he wanted. However, Colin became increasingly uncomfortable with supporting his new man, especially when he found out the man was still associating with past lovers and even other women (as his new man was on the DL in his native country). The requests for money became more and more frequent, in increasing amounts.

Through our work together, Colin got to a place where he knew that he couldn't compromise himself any longer for this man, as there didn't seem to be a future for them for various reasons. At the same time, his ex came back into his life. Colin spoke his truth to his ex and to this day, they are still together and engaged to be married.

MAKEOVER MOMENT:

Whether you are presently in a relationship or not, there are some things that we need to look at and address for ourselves. These things are vital in navigating relationships successfully and powerfully. Here are some things to ponder on now that you are in a relationship:

1. Make a list of those things that are true deal-breakers for you. What are you not willing to compromise? For example, I can't be with an active substance user or someone who is doing something illegal for a living.

2. Now, make a list of the things that you would like but can provide some wiggle room with. For example: *I would love a comic book geek who loves crystals and all things metaphysical.*

3. Make an inventory of your past relationships. Where did you compromise yourself for the sake of being in it? What situations caused you to shrink in your power? Where and how did you lose sight of who you are?

4. If you have a history of being in special relationships or are currently in one, how can you make the shift to a holy relationship? How can you be more in the space of love instead of fear?

5. Revisit what you make relationships mean. Be honest with yourself. Once you get very clear on this, you can start to make shifts in your perception of relationships.

It's meditation time once again, folks. Breathe into the following affirmations to seal in your power after doing this work.

"There is no void."

"Relationships don't complete me; they complement me."

"I stay in touch with who I am at all times."

"I advocate for my feelings and needs."

"I can make compromises without compromising myself."

You may think you have arrived now that you are in a relationship; however, a relationship requires its fair share of work. I have found that most of the work is an internal job. When we place our happiness and peace of mind on external things and events, we will be doomed to inevitable failure and disappointment.

One of the key elements of being in a successful relationship is being in your power without stepping on your partner's power. Don't keep track of what your partner does wrong. Take this as an opportunity to look at yourself and how can you be more like the person you want to be with.

Follow me to the next chapter, one that hopefully you will never have to experience but needs to be addressed nonetheless: "Break-Ups ... WTF?"

11

BREAK-UPS: WTF?

---

*"I am never writing a breakup record again,
by the way. I am done with being a bitter witch."*

- Adele

I hope this is the chapter that you don't have to read and can skip over completely. However, no dating and relationship book is complete without addressing the possibility of breakups and how to navigate them while being the person that you want to be with. For the most part, breakups are usually difficult. Even the most amicable ones can be difficult to manage. I will be brutally honest and tell you that I don't think that I have ever handled a breakup well. Therefore, this chapter will be all about what not to do during a break up.

When Fernando broke up with me, I didn't know what to do. I was in a bit of denial as I thought to myself: *I am a catch. He got too scared off. It was too much for him. When he comes to his senses, we will get back together.* At some point, when he said it would not happen, in a very angry state, I cut him out of my life. Then, by way of guilt, since I am a psychologist and a spiritual person, I asked him back in my life as a friend.

It was this back and forth of being buddies, then me being angry with him, then being buddies, etc. That lasted about three months until he sent me a letter stating how grateful he was that I came into his life and that I was a blessing to him and blah, blah, blah. For whatever reason, I asked him to not speak to me for a while, and as of this writing, we have not spoken despite seeing each other while commuting.

I think one of the main reasons why I didn't want to have any contact with him—and still don't want contact with him—is because I want to shield myself from the possibility of getting hurt by him again. This is a recurrent pattern for me that I have only recently become present to. I shielded myself from him to avoid any further pain; however, the pain remained unresolved. So, I attempted to resolve it by channeling Blanche Devereaux from *The Golden Girls* and going through a slew of men to medicate my pain. (It's embarrassing when I sat down and put pen to paper and realized just how many "a slew" was).

I have never judged folks with any moralistic viewpoint on promiscuity and being sexually active. When I saw the slew of men I went through to get over Fernando, I felt this was not the person I wanted to be. While other folks are okay with this behavior, it didn't feel right for me. I was not the person I want to be with. The reality was that no matter how many men I had sex with and no matter how good the sex was (it wasn't always the case, by the way), I was still left with me. No matter what I did, I never sat with my feelings about the breakup, and I continued to try to heal them through external means.

I would like to present to you something I teach my clients and failed to practice myself after the breakup. To my defense, I didn't really flesh out this concept until way after the breakup. I refer to this concept as the Three C's to solve most problems: **Create Awareness**, **Compassionate Witness**, and **Choose Differently**.

The first C in this model is to **Create Awareness**. I remember the old *G.I. Joe* cartoon of the 80's in which they ended every episode with a learning experience. The "Joe" assigned to that lesson would always end it by saying, "and knowing is half the battle." If I do not know I am experiencing something, I won't be able to move forward with appropriate action and will likely be led down the rabbit hole by the ego. The ego will act out on fear. If I do not identify what is really going on, I will act out in ways that are not in accordance with who I want to be.

I take this concept from Dr. Alan Downs and his book, *The Velvet Rage*. He lists one of the skills in living authentically as asking yourself, "What would the man/woman I wish to become do in this situation?" We all have some notion of the person that we want to be. Even though we don't think we are there yet, we do have some vague notion of how we want to feel and what we want our lives to look like. By knowing that, no matter how vague, we can take actions that are more in alignment with who we want to be.

I knew I was feeling anger, pain, and betrayal but I wouldn't identify what was happening at my core. I didn't want to because I am a psychologist and a spiritual coach so I can rise above it. What I was really doing was spiritually and intellectually bypassing the issue. This led to unconsciously acting out with the "slew" of men I ended up with. Of these men, maybe a handful meant anything to me. They were a means to an end to what I thought I was experiencing.

At the core of what was happening, I felt I had failed once again. I was scared I would "never get it right" when it came to relationships and be doomed to be single forever (once again, making relationships my Higher Power). I was scared, but instead, I played the victim and acted with the following mindset: *If Fernando doesn't give me the validation I deserve, then I will get it wherever I can.*

Once I got clear that what I was feeling was fear, I was able to do something more adaptive about it. I finally got what my coach had been telling me since day one: I needed to get wildly okay with who I am. I was now able to go through the other two C's to get to the result I wanted.

The second C is to develop **Compassionate Witness** consciousness. This is a term Dr. Wayne Dyer used in one of his books and a concept that I think we skip almost 100% of the time. I know that in my personal life and my work with clients, we tend to label feelings as good or bad. If we label them as good, we want to do more to feel more of it. If we label them bad, we judge it harshly and want to do something to control or eliminate it.

Here is where the Compassionate Witness consciousness comes in. Once I have created awareness around what is really going on, I don't judge it. I make it something outside of myself so that I can gain a more objective view on it. Once I make this very subjective experience an objective one, I can then stand in the space of non-judgment and just be compassionate towards it. By doing this, I can witness the emotion and thought and not want to have to do anything about it to change it, increase it or decrease it. No need for self-medication or acting out behavior. I don't own it. I am just witnessing it.

The last C is to **Choose Differently**. Now, I know most of us have a level of self-awareness that we don't always acknowledge. We know what we are capable of doing when we are in a bad space. By practicing the first two C's, we can decide to choose a different course of action, one that is in alignment with who we want to be.

During any breakup (unless it is a super amicable one) we want to do something about it. We want to undo it. We want to forget it. We want to change their minds. We want to know the why. We want to know the answer to "What am I going to do now?" Healing from a breakup will take time. We can feel the pain, have compassion towards it, and take actions that are more in alignment with who we want to be.

Now, these actions are not as immediately gratifying as the actions we want to take *right* now (i.e., the slew of men I went through to numb my unrecognized fear); however, the results of delaying gratification is certainly the better solution. While I don't judge myself today for what I did, I do grimace at my actions back then.

One thing to remember about choosing differently is that it is not always an action we need to take. We could choose differently by not doing something such as not acting on the compulsion and thought to have meaningless sex with a slew of men. It may be we need just to sit down and relax. Inaction can also be a different choice to make with regards to my Three C's.

I also want to talk about some other factors in breakups that I think can be a massive problem. The first one is our fixation on the "why?" I know that this plagued me for quite some time. Since I wasn't in a space to practice the Three C's, I just kept wondering, why did Fernando dump me the way he did? *Why would he want to break up with me? Why is this happening to me? Why do I have to be single again? Why am I not good enough for him?*

One of the things I am very stern about with my clients is that the "why" is not as important as the "what" am I going to do now. I use the example of smoking cigarettes. I knew the why of why I smoked cigarettes. However, the why did nothing to create any lasting change. It wasn't until I was fed up that I was able to quit smoking cigarettes. Knowing the why is applicable and important to know for most problems. Yes, it will provide some relief, but ultimately doesn't do a whole heck of a lot to create change.

The other factor that comes into play here is trying to work through our sense of powerlessness (especially if we were the dumpee versus the dumper), and regain control. I know one of the factors that fueled my "slew" of guys was wanting to feel in control after the breakup. There was also a lot of powerlessness I felt during the relationship because I gave him my power.

Miracle Moment:
Acting out to gain a sense of power only increases our sense of powerlessness.

Think about it: I do something to regain power that really doesn't give me power, and I give it power. I perpetuate the cycle of powerlessness. I create more of what I didn't want because I need to control instead of being compassionate towards it. Follow the 3 C's as outlined above and see if that doesn't give you more power.

Another factor that makes breakups so difficult is the desire to exact revenge on the person. I think this relates closely to control strategies. This person hurt us, so we want to hurt them. However, is revenge really the thing in most alignment with who you want to be?

Think back to the last time you did something mean to someone, whether intentional or not. How did you feel in the long run? Not good, I would imagine. They say the best revenge is living a good life. I feel this gives the most long-lasting effects without the nasty side effects of revenge seeking behavior.

The whole notion of immediate gratification and control are the main reasons why I have stayed in the problem of mismanaging my breakups. I never had the insight to identify what I was feeling in relationships. I pulled the victim card, which just led to a downward spiral. I did not acknowledge my sense of powerlessness and fear; just grasped at whatever came my way to gain a sense of control. These things just led to behaviors that are not me.

Kudos to those who can do it and feel totally within their power. For me, such was not the case. I wanted to feel anything else other than what I was feeling. I did not want nor choose to delay gratification. I wanted to feel good and in control right now. Alas, this just delayed the healing.

One of the best ways to reframe breakups is to see where the learning experience is in the former relationship. *What are your takeaways to make your next relationship better as well as make yourself better?* In a chain email I received once, it said relationships come into your life for a reason, a season, or a lifetime. Let's look at what we can learn from each of these.

Everything has a reason. We do not live in a chaotic universe. There have been many times when even the smallest of encounters led to something very profound. This one time in 2013, I was in a restaurant, eating alone and moping about an ex who was playing with my head once again (or was I allowing it?). The waiter was this stunning man, very Shemar Moore, only taller and more muscular. He was friendly, and we started to chat about self-help books. When he handed me the check, he had written at the bottom of the check, "Keep Rising." When I asked him why he wrote that, he said, "I just want all my customers to leave here and remember to keep rising." There are no coincidences in life, and this chance meeting was presented to me to remind me to stop moping and "keep rising."

Relationships that last a season can have their ups and downs. They may seem like these are relationships we want around for a lifetime; however, that is not their purpose in our lives. I feel strongly that my relationship with Fernando was only ever meant to last for a season. Fernando has been one of my greatest learning experiences of my life and the relationship birthed this book. I was meant to be with him for a short period to get to a greater level of love and acceptance in my own life.

While he and I don't interact at all these days, I am forever grateful that I blossomed into the person I am today, and our relationship was the catalyst for chrysalis. Fernando also verbalized how much he learned and grew from our relationship. The good thing about hitting an emotional rock bottom is that you have nowhere else to go but up.

Lifetime relationships can be a bit of a double-edged sword. These types of relationships can involve family members or friends. This form of relationships offers continual opportunities to learn and grow, whether we like it or not. There is a reason these relationships are in our lives for a lifetime. We learn from all of them.

The bottom line is, regardless of the type of relationship, we will learn. We have no choice in this matter. What is up to us is whether we learn from a space of love or a space of pain. We choose that part. For months after my breakup with Fernando, I was learning from a place of intense pain. Once my head cleared, I was able to see the curriculum that was in front of me all along.

CASE STUDY

Sylvester, the Man with Three Breakups and No Why's

Sylvester was in this cycle of an on again/off again relationship with someone I felt was a total narcissist. After the third breakup, Sylvester was in my office in much pain and insisting on knowing why his former partner did this to him for the third time. He felt that by knowing the why, he would be able to heal faster and move on.

My work with Sylvester consisted of teaching him mindfulness strategies to let go of his need for control and gain a sense of power. Instead of focusing on the why, I coached him on getting present to the "what" now. What can he do right now, despite the pain, to start the healing process without having to know why his partner broke up with him?

The reality was that the breakup occurred. What can he do today to be the person he wants to be? By doing this, Sylvester was able to finally (though with some resistance) let go of the need to know why and identify steps to begin the healing process despite what was (or wasn't) going on externally.

MAKEOVER MOMENT:

Here you are, single again. *What is there to do now?* This is a space in which we can do so much work on creating the possibility of being the person we want to be with. We don't need a breakup for that; however, use this time to get the curriculum you need to move forward. Here are some things that you can do to manage breakups in more adaptive ways:

1. What triggers a sense of powerlessness for you?

2. What safety measures can you implement when you feel powerless so you can act in ways that are more in accordance with who you are/want to be? In other words, how can you leave the victim mentality behind and be the victor?

3. What are your immediate gratification/control strategies? Then ask: What have been the consequences of when you have engaged in these strategies?

4. What are some ways in which you can stop and think more objectively about what the lesson in this rather painful experience could be?

5. Who do you want to be in any given situation? Do you want to be a person who exacts revenge and plays the victim card, or do you want to stand in your fullest power despite the pain you are going through?

6. How can you honor your pain and not judge it?

7. Think of any past relationship, whether it is a reason, season, or lifetime type of relationship. Ask yourself, what did I learn from this (these) relationship(s)?

8. In any situation, ask yourself, "What's my curriculum here?"

This work needs some crucial affirmation time. Sit comfortably and affirm your essential truth after the amazing work you did in this chapter.

"I have power over my choices and actions."

"I am not a victim."

"I can have compassion for my feelings and not judge them."

"I see the lesson behind all of life circumstances."

"Every relationship is an opportunity for growth and change."

Yes, breakups can often suck ass. There are ways in which we can manage the aftermath of the breakup and still stay within our personal integrity. We don't have to worry about the why or for any other external factor to make us happy. We can choose to be happy by applying the concepts in this chapter. We can be in our fullest power if we do so. Every relationship is a learning experience. See what the lesson is, no matter how bad the breakup was. You can grow from this.

Hopefully, this is not a chapter you needed to read. However, it is important to address, as it is part of dating and relationships sometimes, not all the time. So join me in the last chapter where you get to see how you can potentially live "Happily Ever After."

12

HAPPILY EVER AFTER

"Maybe it's a fairy tale, but I believe in happily ever after."

- Jennifer Aniston

It's time to talk about the steps we need to take to move forward once we have become the person we want to be with. Living happily ever after has nothing to do with the person at your side, and it has everything to do with how you feel on the inside. I have seen many relationships that look great on the outside, but inside one or both parties are miserable.

What do we do to live happily ever after, then? Here is the good news and the bad news: The work never stops. However, it does become more second nature the more we practice these skills. The result will likely be that you are living more authentically, more mindfully, and more consciously. The work is ever evolving as well so just be open to the learning experiences that may present themselves. Much like the Buddhist philosophy of non-attachment, our lives (single or coupled) are never exactly how we envision them to be.

Let's review some of the key concepts we have already discussed (and successfully implemented in our lives); however, applying them to the present moment. This can occur in the instance in which you have either done much of the work and are not in a relationship just yet but have created the space for it to come in. Or it can occur when you are in an intimate relationship, and you don't want to lose sight of the work that you have done. The principles discussed in the first eight chapters of the book, as well as some of other principles scattered throughout Chapters Nine, Ten, and Eleven, can be applied on a daily basis regardless of your relationship status.

While you are in a relationship, it is paramount that you continue to keep in mind that relationships are not our Higher Power and we need not make them our Higher Power. I have seen so many people let their own needs fall by the wayside because their whole focus is on the relationship. They lose touch altogether with their friends, or they stop going to the gym or any other self-care practice, because the relationship becomes the only priority in life. Relationships are meant to complement our lives, not complete them. By putting your needs AND your partner's needs at the forefront of your daily lives, you will be living more mindfully.

Know your values, know what's important for you, and know your worth. Regardless of who you have at your side, you still need to maintain self-care and practice the principles that are an essential part of who you are. While compromises do need to occur in relationships, don't ever compromise what is important to you. By making sure we put enough focus on ourselves, we stand in our highest truth. Nothing is sexier than a person who is authentically in their power.

While you are in a relationship, things will come up for you (and likely for the other person as well). Don't judge what comes up. Practice the principle of getting totally okay with who you are in the present moment. Our areas of growth will come up against our partner's areas of growth, and that is okay. Being in a relationship sometimes requires new ways of being that we haven't had much practice with. Don't let your past ways dictate the person you want to be today. You are not that person anymore if you have done the work.

By being aware this may very well happen, we are not caught off guard. Many times, when stuff comes up for me, I want to judge it harshly or eliminate it somehow. The best thing to do is to honor it and see how you can use this to grow. Use the Three C's of managing any situation: Create Awareness, Compassionate Witness, and Choose Differently. The first step in any problem is to know what the problem is by identifying it. Then, you just observe it from a very objective perspective. Don't judge it. Just have compassion about what is there. This way you will be able to do something productive about it. By following these first two steps, you can then choose a course of action in alignment with who you want to be.

Stuff from your past may come up. This may be something you haven't yet made peace because you were not present to it. Relationships do have a way of bringing up stuff for folks, and it is perfectly okay if that happens. What isn't okay is to ignore it or judge it as bad. These things may come up for our continued growth. They are not inherently good or bad; they just are.

Things that may also come up from our past that we would prefer to have buried forever. The issue isn't what happened in the past but who are we today as a result of it. We have all done things we are not proud of; however, they don't define who we are today. They were defining moments in our lives. We don't have to emotionally vomit to our partners every dark detail of our pasts necessarily. If things do rear their ugly heads, we face them and just have a dialogue about it. No need to run from it.

Don't ever compare your relationship with someone else's relationship. If only I had a dollar for every time I have seen this happen, or done it myself, I'd be a billionaire. You are in your relationship, not in someone else's. Your relationship is going to be different than the one you are comparing it to because you are all different people. While you can certainly see aspects of someone else's relationship and want something similar for your relationship, you can't clone it. I've heard many people say, "Comparison is the thief of joy."

Remember when we were growing up and we would compare ourselves to our peers? Remember how miserable we felt because we thought we would never measure up? Well, this will happen when you compare your relationship to someone else's. Be present to what is in front of you right here, right now. Observe it objectively and not from a comparison viewpoint. If there is something you want to change about your relationship, then present that to your partner.

If there is something that you don't like about your relationship and it doesn't look like it can change, then where can you practice some acceptance? Is it a deal-breaker for you? These are the questions to ask. Telling yourself that so-and-so's relationship is "better" than yours does not lead to any positive outcomes.

It is crucial in life to surrender outcomes on a daily basis. This can happen with simple things like riding the subway in New York City to your partner not getting you a Valentine's Day present. As previously mentioned, it is not our desire for things that cause heartache and discomfort, but our attachment that causes misery.

Yes, please have some vision of what it is that you want, but don't hold on to it so tightly that the claw marks remain on the door frame. I have heard it said in Twelve Step fellowships many times, "If you want to hear God laugh, make plans." I don't think our Higher Power *doesn't* want us to make plans, however, let's not to be so fixated on how something is supposed to look like that we have no flexibility in our thoughts about it. Fernando looked great on paper; however, in a real-world scenario, he wasn't the perfect match for *me* that I initially thought he was.

Remember that you don't need to be in a relationship but that you want to be in a relationship. Relationships complement our lives; they don't complete our lives. Every relationship is an assignment, and it's up to us to see what the lesson in this relationship is. Sometimes it's being in a sixty-nine day relationship that ends up being the catalyst for a book on being the best version for yourself, or some other lesson.

I want to have relationships in my life so I grow, change, and evolve. I don't want to be coasting through life. It is thanks to not being in relationships that I learned how to be wildly okay with who I am and not need someone at my side to complete my self-worth. I can truly say I love myself and my life while acknowledging where I still want to be in the future in full acceptance of my present.

Be present and show up for your own life and your relationship, making sure you are always here in both areas equally. I think a lot of times folks lose themselves in relationships once they are in them. Or conversely, they lose sight of the relationship because they are in a state of "Oh well, I've got them already," or even just not being mindful in your relationship. Living life robotically doesn't elicit feelings of vitality and energy.

Miracle Moment:
Show up for yourself, your partner, and
the world. We need your light. Shine brightly.

I look back on this journey in writing this book and respect the growth that has come from it. Of course, going back to old ways of being is quite familiar and by default, comfortable. I feel that doing this work is getting through the discomfort and getting to the other side. It is much like working out. It may not be pleasurable as you engage in it, but the results are amazing.

Doing the work to live "Happily Ever After" reminds me of one of my fave lessons from the Course, which is Lesson 75: "The Light Has Come." After doing this work, we are free from the chains that bind us to dysfunctional ways of being. We are now free to be in our power and ultimately be the person whom we want to be with. I feel very strongly that once that happens, we create the space for that person to come into our lives.

Will it be without its share of issues? No; however, we have better tools and are better prepared to manage them more effectively.

Self-love is always within, and by recognizing it, we will be free and live happily ever after. We will live knowing there are no problems. We will be at peace with ourselves and with the world because we no longer perceive ourselves in a state of lack. We will have an amazing relationship with ourselves because we know we are whole and complete. Old ways of being fade away as our light emerges and we stand tall, soaking in the life experiences relationships offer us. We will be free to love others and ourselves fully. *Isn't this what happily ever after ought to be?*

While most of the chapters have included stories about clients, I want to share with you the greatest lesson about love that I have learned and it only just happened recently. Having done the work that I have written about created the possibility for this invaluable lesson to happen. For me, this was the final lesson I needed to know in this journey on how I can live happily ever after, whether I am single or in a relationship.

In 2008, as I was at the beginning of a very dark period of my life, an amazing kitten entered my life. Since I name all my animals after comic book characters, I decided his name would be Logan. Now Logan was not the prettiest kitten in the world, but as we bonded, he grew to be almost like my biological child. He is a special cat and in many ways, my spirit animal. Logan has also grown up to be a very good-looking cat (and he knows it and reminds me on a regular basis).

He was one of my few constants during a very rough time. Logan made me laugh with his antics when I felt I had nothing to laugh about. He gave me unconditional love when I felt that I was unworthy of this type of love from anyone. This cat has been one of my greatest relationships, and today, one of my biggest learning experiences when it came to truly loving others and myself.

In March 2017, he became very ill over the course of several weeks. I did not recognize the signs of what was going on with him and thought that he was just being Logan and acting out by drinking excessive amounts of water and not grooming. I finally took him to the vet, and he was diagnosed with diabetes. Being a single man responsible for giving twelve-hour insulin injections seemed quite daunting, but I rallied my internal warrior to nurse him back to health. He never gave up on me, so I was determined not to give up on him. I thought he was doing well; however, two months later he became very ill again and needed to be hospitalized. Logan had developed ketones in his urine, pancreatitis, and swollen kidneys. He almost died. After a four-day hospitalization, he came home.

The following day, I looked at him and was just in the space of love for this animal who has been my companion for so many years and so many of the transformational experiences of my life. I looked at how beautiful he was and how much he has come to mean to me. He gave me one of his looks but allowed me to continue to pet him. As I was doing so, I said to him, "*Papi*, if you have to go then go. I let you go. But please stay if you can. I need you around a little while longer."

When I told Logan he could go, I truly felt it and tears came to my eyes. But at that moment, I realized what love truly was. I can love you and let you go if that is what is in the plan. I don't have to hold on to dear life so someone won't leave me. I realized that despite the pain of losing my boy, I would overcome it and march forward. Most of all, I knew I had so many years of giving and receiving love from this animal, and that was the learning assignment.

This was when I realized I was ready. I was now the person I wanted to be with because I didn't have to hang on to something or be someone I wasn't. I just needed to be present and be in the space of love so I could give and receive love. This one experience with my eight-year-old diabetic cat led to the recognition of the love that is, and has always been, present in my life.

Today, Logan is alive and well. Logan loves to throw shade on a daily basis yet cuddles with me at bedtime. He dominates my life as he requires twelve-hour insulin shots and has special dietary needs. As much as I complain about this, I am happy to do it. Don't all relationships require attention?

...

Thank you for taking this journey with me. I channeled this book with information I felt called to put out there. I hope this serves you in getting you to be the best version of yourself that you can be so you can then create the space to bring someone else in as your equal. My desire for a relationship is that it be loving and mutually reciprocal. Without doing all this work, relationships will often be unbalanced and a source of much pain (despite there being a learning experience there for you).

My fondest wish for you is that you successfully take and continue the journey to be the person you want to be with.

- Dr. Tony Ortega

AFTERTHOUGHT

You may have some questions about Fernando at this point and wondering why there really hasn't been any documented closure about this situation that prompted the creation of this book. If I am healed from this situation, why aren't we on better terms? This is hard to write about as my purpose in writing this book was never about bashing him and I won't do so now.

When Fernando and I broke up, I was very angry. I wanted him out of my life and acted in ways and said things that were not in accordance with who I want to be. I got my head somewhat together and decided to have him back in my life. We would even interact on a weekly basis. I bumped into him on the train one day as I was going to my favorite writing spot in the city and told him about the book. Eventually, I came to realize that I was spiritually bypassing my feelings by being so friendly with him.

Throughout the course of my healing, I got present to a lot of things. Some of these things are documented in this book on how I was not the person I wanted to be with during my relationship with Fernando. However, I also got present to some of the problems on his side of the street that I was not allowing myself to see as I was continually making myself wrong.

Around that time, Fernando wrote me a very lovely letter. As lovely as it was, it triggered something in me and I felt like I woke up. Objectively, I got that it was best that we did not interact for sometime. I know that I needed to heal and felt that maybe he needed some time to heal. I thanked him for the letter and also requested that we not speak for a bit.

That "bit" has now been about a year and a half. We have bumped into each other on at least two occasions and neither one of us has acknowledged the other. You would think that this leads to the conclusion that I have not healed. On the contrary, I feel that I have. Not having contact with him is loving myself and being the person I want to be with.

I heard it said that, "Sometimes the loving answer is no." As of today, I say no to a relationship with Fernando, not because I am a bitter, jaded queen but because I make active choices today about who I want in my life. I feel that it is best that we are not in each other's lives. Fernando was never meant to be my "Forever Guy" but my guy for a brief period of time. He was meant to teach me so many amazing lessons that not only birthed this book but also made me into a much stronger individual today. When I think of him, I send him so much love and gratitude.

Namaste,
Dr. Tony Ortega
September 9, 2017

#ISHEHEREYET-
APPENDIX FOR SELF-CARE

As I have mentioned before, it is of utmost importance to engage in a regular practice of self-care. Part of being the person you want to be with is to take care of yourself. If we are to attract the person we want to be with, wouldn't we want to be someone who takes care of themselves? I thought so...

What I have compiled here is a list of activities that you can pick and choose from for your self-care. They are separated into mental, emotional, physical, and spiritual techniques. I am also including a section I call "Utility Belt Tools" (cue *Batman* theme song now). The reason why I have called them Utility Belt Tools is similar to Batman's utility belt. These are things that we can pull out quickly when we don't necessarily have the time to use some of the other ones.

As always, please use and tweak any of these techniques to your liking and lifestyle. For instance, I have never been able to get into yoga yet can do cardio or Pilates until the cows come home (not really, but you get my drift). So, onward my warriors—here are your tools and techniques to be the person you want to be with.

Mental / Emotional / Physical

· **Affirmations** - I always teach my clients (as well as practice myself) how to create great affirmations that work for you. I always recommend making simple phrases that start with "I am." By using the words "I am," you affirm anything that follows it. You can say things like, "I am powerful. I am calm. I am serene." Use your affirmations repeatedly until you feel differently.

- **Mantras** - A mantra is a little different than an affirmation. A mantra does not necessarily start with "I am." This can be anything from one to a few sentences of something you have read or a quote from your favorite author/performer/etc. I will use mantras from *A Course In Miracles*, Gabby Bernstein or Marianne Williamson as my go-to's.

- **Reading** - Read something positive. There are a lot of daily meditation or "thoughts of the day" books out there. Grab one. If you have a smartphone, download a reading app and keep positive literature on there to read.

- **Essential Oils** - Anyone who knows me knows how much I love essential oils. The first thing to do is find a quality essential oil company that works for you. I, personally, only use doTerra oils. I have single oils that I love to work with when I am in a funk, such as Juniper Berry, Arborvitae, Lavender, Frankincense, and any of the more citrusy oils. However, when I am in a playful / experimental mood, I enjoy making blends. I will consult my naturopath or my fave essential oil book then and go to town. There is always a bottle of essential oils within arm's reach.

- **Try Taking a Salt Bath** - This is something that I don't do every often because of my hectic work schedule; however, something that works very well. Get yourself some Epsom salts or some of those pink salt materials and add them to your bath (you can also add some essential oils. Adding Lavender to my salt bath makes me feel so good). Definitely a go-to when you have the time.

- **Take a Walk in Nature** - Again, not something that I do as often as I would like living in the concrete jungle of NYC. However, I am a water person, and hearing water running works when walking in nature doesn't. Maybe have a plant in your office / living environment. Have something accessible that is related to nature around if you are stuck in a concrete jungle like myself.

- **Mindfulness Based Stress Reduction Breathing** - A great way to calm the F down is to practice breathing and mindfulness based stress reduction breathing is so effective. It's quite easy.

All you have to do is inhale to the count of 8, hold to a count of 4, exhale to a count of 8, and hold to a count of 4. Rinse and repeat. Continue this cycle as long as you have to.

· **A Good Shower** - Never underestimate the power of a good shower. This book started in the shower one morning in 2016. Make it as cold or as hot as you want. This is your time. A Ukrainian lover of mine once shared with me a practice in his country where you would change the temperature of the water from hot to cold every 10 seconds to really get you going (I tried it once; not a huge fan, but thought I would share).

· **Exercise** - A good workout always does it for me. When my trainer wakes up inspired, I am a happy camper. I also love doing some cardio on the elliptical watching one of my shows on my tablet. Such a great way to nurture your body and work out some stress (and sex is also exercise, by the way).

· **Massage** - This is one of my favorite things to do to treat myself. I personally love a good deep tissue massage to get the kinks out. (And having a hot masseur is an added plus.)

· **Reiki Session** - Nothing is more relaxing than a good Reiki session. A Reiki practitioner channels universal life energy that is already there. They are just a channel, and this energy can be used to heal all that ails you.

· **Therapy / Coaching** - I regularly see a coach (as I can't see a therapist, since I am one myself) and love it. If you get a good one, they will simultaneously call you on your stuff while providing an environment of support. These services provide you with an objective point of view, which we all need.

· **Travel** - While I am not a big traveler, I do enjoy going to my comic cons as often as possible. Even a day trip can do wonders to disconnect from your day-to-day life. Go somewhere and enjoy yourself.

· **Music** - I personally love music and making playlists. I have my power playlist, my meditative playlist, my positivity playlist, and spoken word playlist. I hear podcasts are a thing now as well. Always have some sort of music going on.

Spiritual

· **Prayer** - With prayer, I personally do not engage in anything formal like I had to in the religion I was raised in. What I like to do is have a conversation with the God of my understanding (or other deities) like I would any other person. In those quiet and calm times of prayer, I get a lot out and sometimes feel the direction that I need to go in. Make prayer as personal as possible.

· **Meditation** - There has been a ton of research on the benefits of meditation. Don't be scared of it. You can make it as simple or as complicated as you want. Start with spending 3 minutes every morning when you first wake up and focus on your breath. If any thoughts come up, just let them be. They will pass if you let them.

· **Angel Therapy** - I personally love working with angels in my spiritual practice. Doreen Virtue has two awesome books on angels—*Angel Therapy* and *Archangels and Ascended Masters*—that you can refer to. You can call upon them to assist you with virtually any problem.

· **Light Bath** - Take a moment and pretend that you are being bathed in healing light. You can be sitting or lying down. Add some colors to it if you want to, but something soothing please. This is one of the ways that you can relax in a quick fashion anywhere you are.

· **Crystals** - I love, love, love crystals. Not only do I wear them but I also have them in my pocket and my bag at all times. I am a tad obsessed. If this is something you want to explore, go to your local crystal shop and pick something that really speaks to you. My go-to's are Hematite, Garden Quartz, Amethyst, and Black Tourmaline. I prefer smooth and tumbled stones to rough. I hold them in my hand or rub them between my fingers as almost a grounding tool.

· **Burn Sage or Incense** - Sage is amazing way to cleanse your house and if you don't mind the borderline pot smell (at least for me), it's kind of amazing. Incense also does wonders for me. Sage and incense are wonderful tools to cleanse any bad juju out of the environment you are in or just change the smell in the air. I am definitely more of a scent person.

Utility Belt Tools

· **Breathing** - When in a jam, the simplest and easiest thing I can pick up is breathing. We forget to breathe sometimes. By just taking deep breaths and focusing on those breaths, we will improve our mood dramatically.

· **Affirmations** - Have a few I AM affirmations ready at your disposal.

· **Mantras** - Have at least one mantra at your disposal. I usually use, "Peace begins with me" repeatedly.

· **Medicine Bag** - You can have some fun in the preparation of making your medicine bag. I also carry in my pocket a bag with some crystals and a special coin. In a pinch, I can reach into my medicine bag and hold a crystal and breathe and affirm. In my regular bag that I always carry, I have some essential oils (some for grounding and some to deal with poor hygiene issues—not mine, however).

· **Light Bath** - (Refer to previous page).

ACKNOWLEDGEMENTS

F and foremost, thank you to the God of my understanding, my Higher Power, without which I have and know nothing.

To Jorge Hidalgo: Thank you for taking this very dark child under your wing so many years ago and starting the process of transforming a lost soul into a powerful man. Words will never express my gratitude for your generosity and love.

To Marianne Williamson: Thank you for introducing me to A Course In Miracles. Those early years, I devoured everything you wrote and listened to as many lectures (and repeatedly) as I could. You are the most amazing and powerful teacher I have ever known.

To Gabby Bernstein, my friend, teacher, and sister: What can I say, girl? I am everything I am because you loved me. You saw what I didn't see and now it's here and evolving constantly. Thank you for everything that you are.

To Joel Readance: You are a handprint on my heart that will be there forever. You ignited a light in me that has led to the most amazing transformations. I have my best life today and it was all because of your unconditional love and truly enlightened tutelage. I love you.

To my Spirit Junkie community (way too many of you to name individually. You know who you are): Guys, you are my community, my tribe, and my family. Thank you for the laughs, shoulders to cry on, and escapades that cannot be discussed publically. I love you guys with all my heart. If friends are a reflection of oneself, then I am simply amazing.

To Alyssa Florio, my fellow Spirit Junkie coach: Thank you so much for the inspiration for Chapter Eight. I was so stuck at that point and you cleared the blocks. The remainder of this book would not have been possible without you.

To all the guys that I have ever been involved with, including Dean and Mick (and especially, Fernando): Thank you for all of the life lessons that you have given me in my personal development. I wish you all nothing but peace and blessings on your journeys.

To the brave men and women that I have been honored to serve over the past twenty five years as a mental health professional: Thank you for allowing me into your lives. A Course In Miracles says, "To teach is to learn." Thank you for the lessons.

To my teaching partner, John Davisi: Dude, you have the patience of a saint to have put up with all the Fernando break up tears and sundry hook-up stories over our Sunday brunches. But seriously, you are a brother to me and you keep me wanting to always strive to be my best. I love you and thank you. So blessed to be teaching with a shining light like yourself.

To my dear friend and confidante, Mark Dominic: I sometimes think to myself how miraculous our friendship is and the serendipity involved in our initial meeting. You have been an example of unconditional love for me in the time I have known you. You were the first to reach out when Fernando broke up with me and the love you showed that day is forever in my heart. Thank you, Pookie.

To my amazing editor, Alisia Leavitt: When divine inspiration gave me the outline for this book, you immediately gave me the basic foundation to get it going. Your editing skills are amazing and I am so grateful you are part of this journey with me. This book would have been nothing without you. You were the OBGYN and midwife to this book, and look what we gave birth to. Thank you.

To my cat, Logan: You have given me so many laughs over the past eight years and gave me the final lesson I needed to complete this book. You will always be the most amazing pet that I have ever lived with. I love you.

ACKNOWLEDGEMENTS

To my parents, Sonia Martinez and Juan Ortega: Thank you for creating me and raising me with the values that are an integral part of who I am today. My only wish is that I have made you proud just as I am proud to call myself your son.

•••

ABOUT THE AUTHOR

Dr. Tony Ortega is a first generation Cuban American. He is a licensed clinical psychologist and life coach who has been in practice since 1992, currently serving the LGBTQ population in his private practice located in Brooklyn, NY. Tony (along with his teaching partner, John Davisi) is the co-creator of the movement, www.rawsexyspiritual.com - Spirituality for Gay Men.

Tony combines cognitive behavioral techniques along with active coaching and metaphysical principles in his work with his clients. Additionally, Tony provides spiritual life coaching for individuals seeking a different way to live. He works with his clients within these three principles: Rewrite Your Story, Find Your Voice, and Live Authentically.

He can be found at www.drtonyortega.com and on social media as @drtonyortega.

Printed in Great Britain
by Amazon

14576132R00100